THE MI STRATEGY BANK

THE MI
STRATEGY BANK

SECOND EDITION

800+ MULTIPLE INTELLIGENCE IDEAS
FOR THE ELEMENTARY CLASSROOM

Ellen Arnold

Zephyr Press

Library of Congress Cataloging-in-Publication Data

Arnold, Ellen, 1944–
   The MI strategy bank : 800+ multiple intelligence ideas for the elementary
classroom / Ellen Arnold.—2nd ed.
      p. cm.
   Includes bibliographical references and index.
   ISBN-13: 978-1-56976-210-3 (alk. paper)
   ISBN-10: 1-56976-210-4 (alk. paper)
   1. Learning strategies. 2. Learning disabled--Education. 3. Multiple
intelligences. I. Title.
   LC4704.A76 2007
   371.9'0472—dc22   2006031675

Cover and interior design: Sarah Olson
Icons designed by Deborah Farber Isaacson

This book is only as valuable as the input from people like you, real teachers and
real learners, who want to build their toolbox of strategies for success. Please
contact me to let me know which strategies worked best.
Ellen Arnold, Ed.D.
ellenarnold@arncraft.com
www.arncraft.com

© 1998, 2007 by Ellen Arnold
All rights reserved
Published by Zephyr Press
An imprint of Chicago Review Press, Incorporated
814 North Franklin Street
Chicago, Illinois 60610
ISBN-13: 978-1-56976-210-3
ISBN-10: 1-56976-210-4

Printed in the United States of America

CONTENTS

INTRODUCTION vii

    What Is the Purpose of This Guide? vii

    Learners: The Real Experts. ix

    How Does This Guide Work? x

1. STRENGTH-BASED INTERVIEWS. 1

    Before You Begin. 3

    Part 1: Setting the Tone and Gathering
        Strength-Based Information 5

    Part 2: Identifying a Problem 14

    Part 3: Brainstorming with the Team 16

    Part 4: Using Strategies Diagnostically with the Learner 17

    Part 5: Following Up. 22

    Case Study 23

2. MI STRATEGY BANKS 31

    Music Smart: The Musical/Rhythmic Intelligence 32

    Picture Smart: The Visual/Spatial Intelligence 39

    Body Smart: The Bodily/Kinesthetic Intelligence 49

    Self Smart: The Intrapersonal Intelligence. 57

    Word Smart: The Verbal/Linguistic Intelligence 64

    Number Smart: The Logical/Mathematical Intelligence 71

    Nature Smart: The Naturalist Intelligence 79

    People Smart: The Interpersonal Intelligence 85

3. STRENGTH-BASED INTERVENTIONS. 93

    Behavior, Discipline, and Motivation 95

    The Learning Process 119

    Assessment 137

4. HIGHER-LEVEL THINKING SKILLS. 145

Glossary 151

Bibliography 159

INTRODUCTION

What Is the Purpose of This Guide?

Teaching elementary students who have difficulty learning in traditional ways can be exciting, challenging, and enriching, but sometimes frustrating. Creative and dedicated teachers will try various strategies to discover the best method to help each child. The theory of Multiple Intelligences (MI), developed by Howard Gardner, can shortcut the trial and error often employed to find the best teaching strategy for each child.

The premise of this book is that when you understand the natural and unique strengths of a learner who may be struggling with traditional academic learning, you uncover a range of possibilities that might otherwise be hidden. When you help learners build on their existing cognitive strengths, they often find learning to be easier and a great deal more fun.

Another benefit of this approach is that when students learn to use strategies that match their strengths, they are usually motivated and see success quickly. This leads them to adapt and transfer these same thinking patterns to other learning opportunities. They think of the tasks as fun rather than frustrating.

The purpose of this guide is to help teachers, support staff, and parents to streamline the process of helping students to find ways to be successful in school. You will learn:

* how to use a strength-based interview to identify the child's perceived strengths;

* how to code the child's perceptions into the MI framework;

* how to create a hypothesis about the learner and the types of interventions to try;

* how to use the chapters in this book to identify strategies that build on the child's strengths while working on the skill or behavior that is most problematic for the child;

* how to capture this information in a format that can be used to communicate with other adults who interact with the child;

* how to help the child to understand better his or her own brain;

* how the child can creatively build a strategy bank that taps strengths to work on weaknesses;

* how to provide a language the child can use to effectively *self-advocate* in order to reach mastery and independence;

* how to use this book as a resource for child study teams whose mission is to support children's learning.

Since this book was first written, I have continued to use and refine this method and these materials as teachers provide me with feedback about their students. As I was working on revising this book, I asked many of my elementary school colleagues: "What was missing? What would make this material more helpful? What lessons or topics would you like to see added?" I am grateful to these dedicated professionals for their suggestions, which included the topics of organization, homework, assessment, and self-advocacy. The triggers used in the strength-based interventions were created in response to teacher requests for quick and easy ways to think about differentiation using MI. These quick reminders should help to get your own creative juices flowing, particularly when the child who is struggling has a strength in your area of weakness, which makes it hard for you to be creative. When you see how other people have used their various intelligences, you have additional avenues to explore.

The current interest in *differentiated instruction* (DI) throughout the United States has added more excitement to this approach. As teachers move toward developing a truly DI classroom, they are asking for resources that can help them bridge their students' current levels with the school district's standards-based expectations. I hope that this book can serve as an effective tool helping them reach that goal.

As a practitioner, I have had the joy of following many of the children whose backgrounds and thinking approaches are captured in this book. I have witnessed these strategies being used with elementary students from coast to coast. You can replicate the success reflected in these pages by following this strength-based MI approach.

Learners: The Real Experts

Research on empowered learners tells us that people rarely learn anything new or difficult by using only their areas of weakness. Successful learners have learned, often unconsciously, to adapt any new learning to their areas of strength in order to master new material. For example, when Emma (see the case study on page 23) could not remember words, she learned to use her love of dance to practice movements that reminded her of the letters. She knew hundreds of dance steps and several ballets from start to finish, even though she was only in second grade. When asked whether she thought she would remember the letters and words that she choreographed, she responded, "Well, of course. I danced them, didn't I?"

Most unsuccessful learners are "stuck" trying to use methods that work for other people but that do not work for them. When they try and fail, their confidence and belief in their own abilities are diminished. Learning to use strengths can be the powerful key that allows such learners to learn more effectively.

Some people have said, "Yes, well, this might work with high school kids, but not young children." Wrong! I have interviewed children as young as three, and once did a revised version of it with a nonverbal, autistic five-year-old. It worked! Children are fascinated with learning more about their brains and about thinking and learning, especially when the approach is interactive, creative, and fun. The only difference between using this approach with a first grader and a tenth grader is the level of vocabulary you might use and the number of props you might have available for the student to use. Elementary school children *do* know what works for them. They may not have the vocabulary to communicate it clearly to you in words, but if you listen, they will give you the information that you need.

How Does This Guide Work?

I designed this book as a resource for tutors, teachers, and parents. It is organized by the eight intelligences, with learning techniques that tap into each intelligence under each heading. It incorporates ideas and teaching techniques from literacy materials, emerging reader studies, books on teaching individuals with learning disabilities, and the real experts—hundreds of learners who have shared their stories and strategies with me. Brilliant Brain (a character I created to help children learn about their Smart Parts; see the Bibliography for a listing of these titles) has led thousands of children on reflective tours of their brains, so that they can be more *metacognitive*, more aware of their own brains—how they work and what they can do to make their brains work better.

Scenarios or Abbreviated Case Studies

In the beginning of each of the eight intelligence sections, you will find a short scenario that describes the success of a specific student I've known. In each case, the student was struggling with learning one of the basic skills considered essential in elementary school. The school district personnel or the parents invited me to interview the child to help discover appropriate strategies, because traditional approaches were not working. Each scenario provides you with a context for the child's strengths and the interventions that were most effective in providing "hurdle help" for the child. As you read these thumbnail sketches, you may think, "Oh, this can't be true!" But I assure you, it is! The magic does not always happen this quickly, but it happens often enough that you will be encouraged to continue to use this approach. I hope these miniportraits trigger thoughts of students you know, and hint how similar interventions may be helpful for them.

Characteristics

Each scenario is followed by a short section of characteristics, which were gleaned from my own research. I asked workshop participants, who identified themselves as having an abundant amount of a particular intelligence, what each felt were characteristics connected to that intelligence. When sufficient patterns emerged, I included them in this section.

Strategies

To build the strategy section, I started my research with people who identified themselves as being particularly strong in one type of intelligence. I then asked them about the strategies they find most effective when reading a novel, when taking notes (or when they took notes in school), when trying to remember phone numbers, or when they feel stressed. After collecting hundreds of these ideas, clusters of strategies began to emerge. These are the cores of the strategies section. I was particularly interested in the stories provided by adults who reported having had difficulty in school when they were children, but had successfully learned to compensate for those earlier troubles. What new strategies did they use?

   I then took the same workshop approach to classrooms across the country. I asked children to identify their strengths, through activities and interviews. I listened as they reflected on the kinds of strategies that worked best when they learned things they found easy.

A Word About Strategies

A *strategy* is a process that a person uses in order to solve a problem or master a skill. A strategy is not an activity or a piece of knowledge, but rather the routine of thinking that occurs in order for the material or skill to be mastered and therefore available when called upon later. A strategy can be used across grade levels, across content areas, and sometimes across skills. It provides a way of thinking that allows the person to be successful in the present and to transfer this thinking to a similar task in the future.

Strategy use requires self-awareness (Self Smart). The student must be able to reflect on what is making the learning happen. The learner makes a choice about the "how" of learning while the teacher decides "what" needs to be learned.

Strategy use also requires self-monitoring (Self Smart and Number Smart), because the learner must be able to determine if the behavior is working to accomplish the goal.

Good students are able to identify, use, and evaluate their use of strategies. Poor students are typically strategy poor. They have few strategies, and often use the same ones repeatedly, whether they work or not. By making strategy use explicit whenever we teach, we provide the modeling and reinforcement necessary for our less successful students to know what they can do differently in order to obtain better results.

The Strength-Based Interview

I worked on refining the interview so that it could be used by people who had not received intensive training in its use. This interview has been piloted and used by teachers and graduate students in a wide variety of elementary settings. In many schools, the interview is completed by a classroom teacher or a child study team member, prior to a student's being reviewed by the team. A complete description of the interview and how to complete it is included in chapter 1.

Once a profile of the child's strengths has been determined, it is taken to the team to be reviewed. Team members refer to the compilation of strategies listed in each chapter of this book to gain ideas for building a strength-based intervention plan.

For example, if a student is good at playing the piano, you might refer to "Music Smart: The Musical/Rhythmic Intelligence." The strategies listed will serve as a starting point, and provide ideas and stimulate your thinking about alternative ways to achieve mastery. I hope that you and the child will try some strategies from this list and then, once they work, become fluent at using this intelligence for any tasks that the child finds difficult.

Format

There are a wealth of connections and interventions included for each intelligence. I have targeted five major categories:

1. **General Learning Strategies**

2. **Academic Strategies**
   * Reading
   * Note-taking
   * Writing
   * Spelling
   * Learning math facts

3. **Behavior Strategies**
   * Frustration
   * Conflict resolution
   * Paying attention when listening

4. **Further Resources to Develop This Intelligence**

5. **Homework and Assessment Opportunities**

Lesson Triggers

I have included a new section in this revised edition devoted to lesson triggers. These are excerpts from real lesson plans used by real teachers, to teach real curricula. Each page contains ideas on ways to connect the topic to all eight intelligences. There are more than 50 lesson triggers, ranging from reading comprehension to cleaning your locker to learning to self-advocate. In many cases these include activities or ways for children to connect to the material, rather than strategies. My hope is that these triggers will provide you with ideas on how to differentiate your instruction using multiple intelligences. You do *not* have to teach each lesson all eight ways. However, as you become fluent in all eight intelligences, you will gain confidence in your ability to translate your own lesson into whichever intelligences are necessary in order for all of your students to be successful.

Glossary

The last section of the book is a glossary. Although I tried to get rid of as much educational jargon in the text as I could, there are always terms and abbreviations that need further explanation. The glossary should provide you with enough information either to answer your question or to direct you to a more comprehensive understanding of the strategy mentioned.

1

STRENGTH-BASED INTERVIEWS

Ten Reasons to Do a Strength-Based Interview

1. Every learner is unique and needs ways to celebrate his or her uniqueness.

2. When students lose the belief in themselves, they cannot be successful.

3. Creative learning is *never* boring.

4. The responsibility for learning is the student's responsibility. But before students can take responsibility, they have to know what will work for them.

5. In order to take responsibility for learning, the learner must be metacognitive.

6. One teacher's strategies may not work for the student, even though they may work for the teacher.

7. Students who aren't effective in basic skills don't know what they need to do differently.

8. MI provides a reframe for students, a positive paradigm so they can have hope for success. "Just because you can't do it one way, doesn't mean you can't do it. You just need to do it *your* way."

9. Unsuccessful students are tunnel-visioned in their use of strategies. The regular way didn't work and no one gives them permission to do it in an alternative way.

10. Inappropriate behavior is often a signal of something the student is *good* at:

    * The mover is demonstrating Body Smarts.
    * The doodler is demonstrating Picture Smarts.
    * The talker is demonstrating People Smarts.
    * The one who says "let's get to the point" is demonstrating Number Smarts.
    * The hummer is demonstrating Music Smarts.
    * The arguer is demonstrating Word Smarts.

Your job is to help students identify strengths from their areas of competence, and teach them how to build bridges from those areas to the thinking we want them to develop.

The strength-based interview is conducted in five parts:

Part 1: Setting the Tone and Gathering Strength-Based Information

Part 2: Identifying a Problem

Part 3: Brainstorming with the Team

Part 4: Using Strategies Diagnostically with the Learner

Part 5: Following Up

Before You Begin

Put together a supply of materials or props that will help you conduct a strength-based interview.

ITEM	SOURCE
Plastic brain (or Koosh ball or sponge)	www.neuromart.com
3 x 5 cards, some lined and some without lines	Stationery store
Pipe cleaners (cut in half, to use to fidget or build)	Craft shop
Plastic letters/Scrabble tiles in a divided sewing box	Garage sales
White board and colored markers, or white static paper	Stationery store
Cuisenaire rods or attribute blocks	School supply store
Small, battery-operated tape recorder or digital recorder (to replay the conversation so you can take accurate notes and then share them with parents)	Electronic supply store or department store
Franklin Homework Wiz Spell Checker with read-aloud key	www.franklin.com
Icons of eight intelligences, from page 31, on a small felt board (can be done in the shape of a brain)	Make this for yourself
Brilliant Brain Becomes Brainy! (Rochester, NY: Arncraft, 1997)	www.arncraft.com
Eight toys or 3-D objects to represent the eight intelligences or Smart Parts	Your junk drawer

The strength-based interview requires:

* Usually two sessions with the student, each approximately 20 minutes.
* A space where you are relatively free of distractions.
* A student whose primary issues are cognitive rather than emotional.

When you administer this interview, your job is to really listen. Listen not just to the overall content, but also to the wording and phrasing used, the verbs used, the way the learner describes his or her world. The questions below are meant to be options or prompts to get at the necessary information. You do *not* have to ask all the questions, nor use this exact wording. If you become stuck, the dialogue stimulators below are sure to work, but insert your own personality, your prior knowledge of the learner, or anything you have available to help you get at the key issues:

* How does this learner's brain work best?
* Under what conditions?
* Using which modalities?
* Using which intelligences or associations?

Part 1:
Setting the Tone and Gathering
Strength-Based Information

Goals:

* Set the tone
* Identify the expert
* Have student verbalize individual strengths
* Structure the student into a metacognitive dialogue
* Record (tape or notes) the learner's perceptions and validate the learner's experiences

Breaking the Ice

First, open a dialogue with your interviewee: "Our reason for meeting today is to find out more about your brain and how it works. We all have different ways in which our brains are smart, and I want to find out more about your brain." Alternatively, you can say, "You are the expert on how *your* brain works. I am going to ask you a bunch of questions to get you thinking about how your brain works best. You are free to answer in words or pictures, or to build things with any of the materials on the table." Have materials available from the list on page 3 that may be helpful to the child, such as markers, white board, pipe cleaners, plastic brain, Koosh ball, or other props.

Strengths

Photocopy the form on the next two pages. Use this form to ask questions and to record the student's responses. These questions have been designed to elicit the student's self-perception as a learner. Again, don't feel as if you have to ask every question, but make sure you get enough information to really understand the learner.

If, after you have completed the interview, you have collected a tremendous amount of information, condense what you have onto a fresh page that can be used to share information and plan interventions.

STRENGTH-BASED INTERVIEW NOTETAKING SHEET		
Question	Student Response	MI Hypothesis
What are you good at? How do you know you are good at it? How did you learn it?		
What else are you good at? How do you know?		
What do you like to do? How did you learn it? What do you like about it?		
How do you know when you know something?		
What does your mom or dad say you are good at?		

If you are doing more than half the talking during the interview, you are not getting information from the real expert—the learner. Don't worry if the student talks about things that are not related to school. You are interested in the process of learning—when does it happen best and easiest. For example, the student who has already taken apart and rebuilt car stereos has learned a great deal of information, skills, and procedures. You just need to find out the magic formula for how the student learned it and

Question	Student Response	MI Hypothesis
What would your friends say you are good at?		
What about your teacher?		
What do you like to do after school?		
What is your favorite book?		
Why?		
What was something you learned in school that was easy for you to learn? What made it easy?		
Can you think of something you did in school that made you proud? What was it?		

how he or she remembers it. Later, you can help the student to translate that formula into school-related learning.

Introducing the Student to the Concept of Multiple Intelligences

Have the student use the eight toy props you collected (see page 3) to manipulate and organize responses. You may also use the eight Smart Part icons. You might read the first half of *Brilliant Brain Becomes Brainy!* as an introduction.

First, lay out the eight toys and let the student manipulate them.

Then introduce this material by putting the following quote into your own words.

"Here are eight symbols of the eight ways your brain is smart. All people have all eight of these intelligences in their brains. I want to make sure you understand how each one works, and then I am going to ask you to decide which one your brain is strongest at, and which ones your brain needs to work harder at in order to use them."

Do not teach or lecture about each Smart Part. Let the student tap prior experience or automatic associations as much as possible. Use prompts like the ones found on page 9 if necessary to reframe or provide more information. Then ask what someone would be like if the person had this as a strength.

Use the student's response to check for accuracy in understanding. Encourage questions. Clarify any misconceptions, and add any of the following elements that the student may have left out.

Record a check when you feel the student has a good understanding of a Smart Part.

Once you have determined that the student understands the eight Smart Parts, ask the learner to rank them in order. Say, "Now, I would like to know which ones of these you think are your strongest and fastest Smart Parts, the parts you think work easiest in your brain. Move the toys (or icons) around and put them in the order that you think they work the best."

SMART PARTS CHECKLIST FOR STRENGTH-BASED INTERVIEW		
Smart Part Prompts	**Descriptors & Characteristics**	✔
Which one is Music Smart?	Hums, plays an instrument, learns songs quickly, remembers music easily, writes music	
One of them is Picture Smart. Which one?	It looks like a strange eye because it is not the eye on the outside of your head; it is the one inside your brain. Imagine pictures, use color, design things, draw, doodle, paint, remembers movies or pictures well	
Which one is Body Smart?	Anything using the body, sports, building things, making things, LEGO bricks, blocks, mechanics, sewing	
Which one is Self Smart?	Likes being alone and having time to think, understands self and own thoughts and feelings	
Which one is Word Smart?	Reading, writing, speaking, using vocabulary, spelling, communicating with words	
Which one is Number Smart?	Adding and subtracting, doing problems in your head, learning anything with numbers, organizing things, estimating time, money, liking structure and routine, patterns	
Which one is Nature Smart?	Raising or training animals, communicating with them, gardening or growing plants, interest in ecology or environment, fishing, hunting, taking care of the natural world	
What's left? What does it look like?	Friends, listening, being comfortable with others, thinking better within a group, good at meeting new people, reading others' body language	

Record student choices on the table on page 11.

"Great. Now tell me what evidence you have for each one. For example, you said that _____ was first. Can you tell me why you put it first?"

Continue collecting evidence through all of the Smart Parts, recording the child's responses on the table on page 11.

Frequently Asked Questions About Conducting a Strength-Based Interview

Q: What if students do not understand one of the Smart Parts, which becomes clear when they give evidence?

A: Then reframe and reteach, or say, "That might be part of it, but I was thinking this Smart Part meant . . ."

Q: What if the student has given you a lot of evidence for being one Smart Part in the strengths section, but denies it here?

A: You can say, "I wonder about _____ Smart. I thought I heard you say that that one was really strong when you talked about being good at _____. What do you think?" Alternatively, say, "After listening to you, I wonder whether you may also be _____."

Q: What if the student's order is very different from what the student told you in the earlier interview?

A: Reframe and reteach, but remember: the student is the expert. Try to find out the reason for the student's response. Say, "You told me before that you were really, really good at making friends (or another characteristic), but you rated People Smart near the end. Help me to understand why you rated it that way." Once you have talked about it, allow the student the opportunity to rethink and reorder, but never change the sequence because *you* do not agree.

EVIDENCE OF YOUR SMART PARTS

Smart Part	No. ordered by child	Evidence child provides (Use quotes when possible)	No. of times suggested in interview
Music Smart			
Picture Smart			
Body Smart			
Self Smart			
Word Smart			
Number Smart			
Nature Smart			
People Smart			

Learning Profile

Goals:

* To put the theory of MI in the perspective of the entire learning process

* To gather more information about the way the learner masters new information

In this segment of the interview you are trying to find out modality and output preferences, not just the intelligences used when learning and making connections internally. This often works better when you use the plastic brain. You may use pencils or pipe cleaners for input and output.

Say, "I want to know more about your brain. You have given me a lot of information about how you think and learn, and how your brain can store information, but I need to know a little more about how you learn. I want to know more about the best way to help move things into your brain and the best ways to find out if you really know something."

LEARNING PROFILE QUESTIONS

Questions	Record Student's Response
Do you get information better if you see it or if you hear it? How do you know?	❑ *See* ❑ *Hear*
Once you see it or hear it, and then store it in your brain, what is the best way for you to show what you know? ❑ Tell about it? ❑ Write about it? ❑ Draw it? ❑ Build it? ❑ Act it out?	
Some students have "stop signs" in their brains, where things become stuck. I want to know where your stop sign is. Is it getting things in, understanding and storing them, or getting things out?	❑ *Input* ❑ *Processing* ❑ *Output*
How do you know? Give me some examples.	

Part 2:
Identifying a Problem

Goals:
* For a student to identify one skill or task to be improved
* To formalize the role of strategic intervention with the student

Keep this section of the interview short—only a few minutes. You do not want to dwell on the negative, but you do need the student to identify something to work on, such as a word that is hard to remember, a math fact, or a vocabulary word that is not understood. For older students, it may be organization skills or reading comprehension. Remember, the focus is on strengths, so do not dwell on areas of weakness.

Ask the questions in the chart on page 15, reordering the student's responses.

Summarize Your Interview

Conclude your interview with the student. Say, "I learned so much about you and your brain today. I learned that you are good at _____ and that you are confident using these Smart Parts (point to them). I also learned about the things that are hard for you. Did I get it right? Show me where I went wrong.

"I want to thank you for doing such a good job sharing. I am going to think about all the things I learned about you today. I will do some research on strategies that may be most helpful to you in becoming better at _____, and then I will meet with you again and we can try some things that use your strengths. Is that OK?"

CAPTURE SHEET FOR A STRENGTH-BASED INTERVIEW

Weaknesses	Response	MI
Now that I know things you are good at, are there any things that are hard for you? What makes them hard? Which part is hard?		
Has it always been hard? How do you know?		
What have you tried to do to make it easier?		
What has worked best? Have you tried any strategies to help?		
What one thing do you like least in school? Why?		
What is something you would like to change about your brain or how it works?		

Part 3:
Brainstorming with the Team

In many schools, interviewers use their Child Study Team or Instructional Support Team (or whatever you call it in your building) to *brainstorm* potential strategies that will be effective for interviewed learners.

The interviewer presents:

* The completed Capture Sheet (the one-page summary)
* A hypothesis about the learner's cognitive strengths— what works best, the evidence given by the learner, and other supporting evidence

Then the team members brainstorm ideas that will tap into the learner's strengths as they work on the area(s) of weakness. For example, a Number Smart student who cannot remember how to spell words might start with counting the number of letters in a word, then look for patterns in the word, and then connect the word to a formula.

This book can be used as a resource by members of the team to stimulate conversations about the best possible strategies for this child to use.

If you are not part of a formal building team, create one with colleagues who seem able to reach learners that are hard for you to reach. Such variation indicates that their teaching profile/ learning profile may be different from yours, and therefore their creative and automatic use of strategies may be different. Their ideas and insights should prove very helpful.

Part 4:
Using Strategies Diagnostically
with the Learner

Goals:

* To empower the learner by presenting a strategy that feels safe (because it taps into the learner's strengths)

* To identify whether this strategy can be used at the independent level

* To experiment with the potential success of this strategy

* To measure success of the strategy for you and for the learner

* To demonstrate to the learner that the right strategy influences and can change results

Once strategies have been identified, schedule another session with the learner to do some diagnostic teaching to see how it works. If the strategy really taps the learner's strengths, you should get reactions like "This was fun," or "I like this," or "I can learn this way."

Start by giving directions to the student: "Pick a word (or a number concept, or whatever the learner has identified as a problem) you would like to learn. Since you told me you were a _____ learner, we are going to experiment with a strategy from this Smart Part in order to use your brain's strongest or fastest parts." Help the child to identify a fact, word, concept, or skill.

Next, tap background knowledge or immediate associations. "What does this make you think of? How can you use your

Smart Parts to connect to this? What is one way that you could remember this? What else can you think of?"

This exercise will often stimulate out-of-the-box thinking. You will need to be open-minded and nonjudgmental in order for this to work. Do not censure. Try to suggest strategies that tap the learner's strengths. Remember, the real expert is the learner.

Verbalize the strategy that is being used. Use "think alouds." Review the steps. Try it several times if appropriate. *Scaffold* it or *tier* it (i.e., teach incrementally) to make it successful. Slowly turn over ownership of the strategy to the student, commenting on what you are doing (scaffolding). Make strategy use explicit. Amend the strategy as you gather diagnostic information about the student's ability to use it effectively.

Once it has been mastered, have the student do a "think aloud" or, if nonverbal, draw a *storyboard* or a formula for the steps so that you can verify understanding.

Closure

Goals:

* To obtain closure
* To verify understanding
* To identify next steps

Wrap up your intervention with the student. "I really enjoyed spending time with you and finding out more about your brain. I really liked that we were able to come up with some fun, new ways for you to learn. I just want to summarize what we learned about you and your brain."

Ask the questions in the table on page 19, and record the learner's responses. If you can tape-record the session (which I strongly recommend), you can offer to share the tape with the parents or another teacher, and give a copy of the tape to the child.

CAPTURE SHEET FOR A STRENGTH-BASED INTERVIEW II

Closure Questions	Student's Response
What did you learn about yourself and your brain through this strength-based interview process?	
Did you put any ideas/tools in your toolbox?	
What do you think? What strategies do you want to use after today?	
Whom do you want to share this with? I will write up my notes from our time together and give you a copy so that we both have a record of this. (Use the following Capture Sheet for these notes.)	

Now that you have all this wonderful data from the child, you can compress it in a user-friendly way that can be shared with the student and with the school personnel who will be involved in planning appropriate strength-based interventions. Here are some tips for using the Capture Sheet.

* Fill out the top half (information, student quotes, strengths and weaknesses) based on your completed interview; include two or three of the student's fastest or strongest Smart Parts.

* Fill out the Discussion/Activities section based on your diagnostic teaching with the child.

* Use key words, not sentences.

* Record the student's own words whenever possible.

* Use simple language, not jargon.

* Remember that your audience is the *child* first, then the supportive adults.

* Stay focused on the learner's strengths (this is why the Strengths box is so much larger than the Weaknesses box).

When you are finished, share the completed form with the student to check for accuracy. Then share it with the teachers and staff involved in the building team. After reviewing this document, participants should be able to brainstorm strength-based recommendations. Fill out the Recommendations box at the end of the meeting.

The Results box will be used when you review the case. The time frame can vary from two weeks to six months after the interview.

STRENGTH-BASED INTERVIEW CAPTURE SHEET

Name _____

Interviewed by _____

Date _____

Location _____

Observers _____

STUDENT SAID:

STRENGTHS:

WEAKNESSES:

DISCUSSION / ACTIVITIES:

RECOMMENDATIONS:

RESULTS:

Part 5:
Following Up

**Later—at least two weeks after your interview—check in
with the student to find out:**

* Has the strategy been used?

* How has it worked?

* Does it need to be adapted?

* What is the learner's perception of its effectiveness?

* Is there another problem the student would like to
  work on to develop a strength-based approach?

Then fill in the results box.

Case Study

To help you better understand the strength-based interview, the following pages show a case study and interview conducted with a second grader named Emma.

STRENGTH-BASED INTERVIEW NOTETAKING SHEET		
Question	Student Response	MI Hypothesis
What are you good at? How do you know you are good at it? How did you learn it?	I am creative. I like to use my imagination. I like to make up things, using drawing. I have a lot of friends and love being with them.	Picture People
What else are you good at? How do you know?	I love to dance and do gymnastics and acrobatics and diving. It is fun and other people tell me I am good at acrobatics and gymnastics and dance. I am great at round-offs. I taught myself how to do cartwheels. I watched my friends do it and then I just did it. I can learn new steps fast.	Body People Self People Body
What do you like to do? How did you learn it? What do you like about it?	I like to be with people. I am a good friend. I like it when other people like me. I like to be a helper.	People People

STRENGTH-BASED INTERVIEW NOTETAKING SHEET (CONTINUED)		
Question	Student Response	MI Hypothesis
How do you know when you know something?	I can just tell.	Self
What does your mom or dad say you are good at?	Being fun.	People Self
What would your friends say you are good at?	Being a friend.	People
What about your teacher?	I don't know.	X
What do you like to do after school?	Dance or draw.	Body Picture
What is your favorite book?	I don't have one.	X
Why?	Reading is hard.	X
What was something you learned in school that was easy for you to learn? What made it easy?	Art class. I already know how to draw.	Picture
Can you think of something you did in school that made you proud? What was it?	When I helped my friend when she came back from a trip, and I taught her the math she missed.	People

EVIDENCE OF YOUR SMART PARTS

Smart Part	No. ordered by child	Evidence child provides (Use quotes when possible)	No. of times suggested in interview
Music Smart	3	Music helps me remember the dance steps.	
Picture Smart	2	Drawing, making up fun cartoons. I have movies in my head sometimes, as well as pictures.	5
Body Smart	1	Dance, gymnastics, swimming, acrobatics. I can even make up my own dance steps. I used to be on a swim team and that was fun.	3
Self Smart	4	I know when I am sad and happy. But I don't like to be alone very much.	3
Word Smart	7	I like it when other people read to me, but it makes me mad that I can't remember the words when I try to read them myself.	
Number Smart	5	Math is OK, and I do like to organize my room, but my mom doesn't always like the way I do it because I do it by color and not by where she thinks things should be.	
Nature Smart	6	I don't like spiders and snakes.	
People Smart	8	I am good with friends, helping others, telling how other people feel.	9

CAPTURE SHEET FOR A STRENGTH-BASED INTERVIEW

Weaknesses	Response	MI
Now that I know things you are good at, are there things that are hard for you? What makes them hard? Which part is hard?	Word study is really hard. I get a pink piece of paper with my words for the week. My friends get different colors than me. Sometimes I get headaches when I am trying to do the word study. I can't remember the words when it gets to the test, even if I work on it a lot.	Word Smart
Has it always been hard? How do you know?	Yes, because I always do bad on the tests.	Word Smart memory
What have you tried to do to make it easier?	Copy the words over and over.	Word Smart strategy
What has worked best? Have you tried any strategies to help?	Nothing. Having my mom help me.	People Smart
What one thing do you like least in school? Why?	Reading. It is hard.	Word Smart
What is something you would like to change about your brain or how it works?	Learn words and get them to stick.	Word Smart

CAPTURE SHEET FOR A STRENGTH-BASED INTERVIEW II

Closure Questions	Student's Response
What did you learn about yourself and your brain through this strength-based interview process?	I learned I am smart, sort of.
Did you put any ideas/tools in your toolbox?	Does using color count? And playing games with words?
What do you think? What strategies do you want to use after today?	I want to play these kinds of word games when I have to do word study, instead of the old way.
Whom do you want to share this with? I will write up my notes from our time together and give you a copy so that we both have a record of this.	My mom and dad, and *not* my teacher, because she might be mad. She sometimes thinks I am not trying and she tells me to stop drawing. Can you tell her it is OK for me to draw when I do words?

In a summary letter I wrote to Emma, I included the following recommendations, based on Emma's strengths. I also asked Emma to give a copy to her teacher, and to have her teacher call me if she had any questions. I also made a tape recording of my letter to send to her, so she could listen to my reading of it.

A. **When you are learning something new (like a new word) you need to follow these steps:**
   1. Think of what you already know first.
   2. Look carefully at the letters in the word and their order.
   3. Think of a creative way to remember the parts you do not know already.
   4. Dance (choreograph) or draw something that represents the letters that are in the word (take your time).
   5. Test yourself by looking away; then look back at the card to check it.
   6. Review the word the next day, and think about which strategy seemed to work best in helping you remember it.
   7. Use blue paper or a blue transparency over the page and see whether you have fewer headaches when you are looking at a paper color that is not pink.

B. **Strategies you found helpful when learning to spell a word.**
   1. Put the hard letters in a different color so they stand out.
   2. Draw a picture to remind you of the hard letters.
   3. Make up fun, creative dances, or cheers using the words or the letters that are hard. In my office today you made up some dance steps for the words "what" and "with."

4. Use a white board and a variety of colors to practice writing the words.

5. Keep the words on big flash cards or in a notebook so you can review them. Record the clues you made up on the card as well, so you can remember them better.

C. **Additional strategies you might try.**

1. Learn to do "moving without disturbing" strategies.

   a. Move your weight from one leg to another (without anyone's knowing).

   b. Wiggle your toes inside your shoe without moving your shoe.

2. Think of other moving-without-disturbing strategies that will work for you. Do the *reciprocal teaching* strategy with your mother, father, or friend.

   a. Each of you decides how many words you will each read before you switch who is reading. For example, maybe you will read every third word, and your mother, father, or friend will read the rest. Alternatively, maybe your mother will read seven words and then you will read the next two, then she will read seven.

   b. Now you can read the book together and neither of you has to read for very long.

   c. You can do the same thing with a friend, with each of you reading one word, so you share in the reading equally.

STRENGTH-BASED INTERVIEW CAPTURE SHEET

Name _Emma_

Interviewed by _Ellen Arnold_

Date _11/20/05_

Location _Office in Rochester, NY_

Observers _Mom_

STUDENT SAID:

I love to draw cartoon characters that make other people laugh. I can make friends. Sometimes I get headaches when I am trying to do the word study. I can't remember the words when it gets to the test, even if I work on it a lot.

STRENGTHS:	WEAKNESSES:
Acrobatics, gymnastics, dance Drawing, creative, makes up own cartoon characters People, friends, making them laugh Cares about her work, wants to do better Verbal, seems to know herself well	Words, reading Memory for words she studied

DISCUSSION / ACTIVITIES:

* Strength-based interview questions worked well. She was verbal and self-aware.
* Once we identified her strengths, we used white board, colored markers, and Scrabble tiles to experiment with ways to remember words.

RECOMMENDATIONS:	RESULTS:
1. Colored markers, white board, make up own visuals for words 2. Creative associations (choreograph, draw) 3. Experiment with colored transparencies and markers 4. Reciprocal teaching 5. Keep your own personal dictionary of words learned 6. Share information on strengths with teacher	

2

MI STRATEGY BANKS

MUSIC SMART
Musical/Rhythmic Intelligence

PICTURE SMART
Visual/Spatial Intelligence

BODY SMART
Bodily/Kinesthetic Intelligence

SELF SMART
Intrapersonal Intelligence

WORD SMART
Verbal/Linguistic Intelligence

NUMBER SMART
Logical/Mathematical Intelligence

NATURE SMART
Naturalist Intelligence

PEOPLE SMART
Interpersonal Intelligence

Music Smart:
The Musical/Rhythmic Intelligence

This person likes to:

* connect music to emotions;
* have music in his or her head all the time;
* sing to him- or herself;
* tap or move to rhythms.

Music Smart Scenario

Becky's speaking voice is clear and mellow. She laughs easily and loves to make others laugh. She often hums to herself during class. She delights in creating "silly" rhymes, which gets her into trouble in class. Becky gets along well with others, but her class work is inadequate.

Music Smart Strategies Used

1. Becky is encouraged to make up rhymes using the vocabulary she needs to learn for class.
2. Becky is put in charge of writing a "musical revue" to summarize content.

Results

Becky composes relevant songs and poems. Her teacher creates a positive tone for Becky to orchestrate the engagement of others into the production of the theatrical summary. Becky's passion for music and humor communicates to others as she finds ways to channel her creativity positively. Her disruptiveness in class decreases.

Characteristics of the Music Smart Learner

* Background sound helps concentration and production
* Easily distracted by extraneous sound
* Is relaxed, stimulated, and motivated by music
* Learns best when information is in rhyme, rhythm, tune, or pattern of sounds
* Listens well
* Reacts to voice tone in others
* Relates concepts to rhymes, poems, and music
* Remembers by using songs to understand concepts
* Remembers music and lyrics easily
* Rhythmic in speech
* Strong auditory skills

Music Smart Strategies for Learning

The student who thinks best using patterns of sounds can use the following strategies:

* Associating to sound patterns
* Being conducted by others
* Chanting
* Creating rhymes
* Finding songs with themes similar to content in class
* Hearing music relevant to a topic or time period being studied

* Hearing patterns of words and relating them to the patterns in music
* Humming
* Keeping a beat while reading or writing
* Listening
* Listening to classical music as background
* Listening to music, chants, or nature sounds while writing or drawing
* Listening to sound recordings or using earphones
* Moving to music
* Putting rhythms to words, concepts, or formulas
* Reading notes aloud
* Relating rules of language to the rules of music (tempo, rhythm, rhyme, tone)
* Repeating patterns of sounds and words
* Responding emotionally to music (but often unable to articulate)
* Rhyming
* Singing
* Tape-recording reading aloud and relistening to tape
* Tapping to self while reading a book aloud
* Thinking first and then expressing self through song, orally or in writing
* Vocal chords respond when listening to someone else singing
* Writing music that relates to the mood or theme of the learning
* Writing rap using own ideas and new vocabulary

Music Smart Reading Strategies

* Blending
* *Choral reading*
* *Impress reading*
* Improving fluency by setting to music
* Learning sounds by association to songs
* Listening to poetry as well as prose
* Playing music in background when reading
* Repeating sounds after teacher
* Rereading after someone else models the reading
* Using an auditory phonetic approach; focusing on the sound and sound reproduction
* Using Hooked on Phonics
* Using sounds of words

Music Smart Writing Strategies

* Analyze writing by cadence, tone, or rhythm
* Listen to a selection of music and describe feelings, events, and meanings
* Repeat a *mnemonic* for process writing
* Sing the words and then write them
* Use classical music in the background as a stimulator while writing
* Write about famous musicians
* Write lyrics instead of prose

Music Smart Spelling Strategies

* Count out or tap the number of sounds (phonemes)
* Count out or tap the number of syllables

* Create a song or rhyme to learn the letter sequence
* Identify different instruments to correlate to certain vowels or consonants
* Repeat letters aloud and set to music
* Spell aloud to hear whether the sequence sounds right

Music Smart Math Strategies

* Connect numbers to sound patterns
* Create a song for number facts
* Develop a rap using numbers
* Equate fractions to musical notation
* Identify a letter to go with each number (A = 1, B = 2, etc.) and write the new music
* Learn existing songs about numbers (e.g., *Schoolhouse Rock*'s "Multiplication Rock")
* Master the use of a metronome
* Perform music in sequence
* Tap facts to a rhythm
* Use the sounds of the keypad on a phone to remember formulas
* Write lyrics to a song

Music Smart Strategies to Pay Attention During a Lecture

* Finger tap (without sounds others can hear)
* Foot tap (in the air)
* Listen for rhythms
* Listen to tone of voice or accent of the speaker
* Make up rhymes

* Play music in head
* Sing in head
* Trumpet-fingering while listening

Music Smart Note-Taking Strategies

* Develop abbreviations that use musical notation
* Practice skills by listening to lyrics and writing them in personal shorthand
* Remember information through word associations
* Take notes in rhymes, poems, or songs
* Tape information

Music Smart Strategies When Frustrated

* Be featured in a talent show
* Be rewarded for good behavior with music
* Connect with a musical advocate or mentor
* Do a music inventory for the school
* Find jobs in the school related to music or sound effects
* Listen to a recording or use earphones
* Research the kinds of music that calm people down
* Think of a song that changes personal moods
* Write raps about preventing fighting and violence

Music Smart Conflict-Resolution Strategies

* Design an orchestra where the members solve conflicts
* Find other songs that have fighting or conflict resolution as the theme (i.e., "Peter and the Wolf")
* Identify patterns of behavior and translate them into patterns of music (i.e., conflict, resolution of sound)

* Write and perform a rap about the events and conclusion
* Write music that demonstrates the feelings of peaceful resolution

Resources for the Music Smart

* CDs, MP3s, audiotapes, iPods
* Children's music
* Commercials on television
* Lyrics
* Orff instruments (which create sound patterns)
* Mozart
* Music composition books to write in
* Musical instruments
* Musical theater
* Nursery rhymes
* Poetry
* Raps
* *Schoolhouse Rock*
* Songbooks
* Theme songs

Picture Smart:
The Visual/Spatial Intelligence

This person likes to:

* do puzzles;
* draw;
* imagine;
* use color;
* visualize.

Picture Smart Scenario

Henri loves to draw very detailed pictures and has a vivid imagination. He loves fantasy games and being read to. Henri cannot remember which direction letters are supposed to go. He daydreams in class and is falling further behind. Spelling and reading are below grade level.

Picture Smart Strategies Used

1. Henri is asked to create shapes for the letters he finds confusing.
2. He uses colored markers or pipe cleaners, and is given freedom to come up with visual associations that work for him.

Results

He decides to make the silent *e* look like the graphic below to remind him of a tent that is "outside of the rest of the word, like a tent is outside of the house."

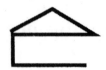

He could not remember the difference between "in" and "on," so he made the following shapes on his own.

Henri's mother bought him a set of pipe cleaners and a white board with colored markers, and his sight word vocabulary and spelling improved markedly.

Characteristics of the Picture Smart Learner

* Creates images in mind's eye
* Describes things in vivid detail
* Dreams frequently in color
* Enjoys using *graphic organizers*
* Has a "file of index cards" in mind
* Learns through connecting images
* Needs to see information
* Prefers having a model
* Remembers pictures better than words
* Sensitive to color

* Strong sense of direction
* Thinks through a design or process with the assistance of visuals
* Thumbs through pictures stored in mind
* Turns shapes around internally
* Uses maps rather than sequential directions

Picture Smart Strategies for Learning

The student who learns best through seeing or visualizing could use the following strategies:

* Cartooning
* Creating a storyboard
* Creating and building jigsaw puzzles
* Creating pictures in the mind while listening to someone talking or while reading
* Color-coding notes or a story
* Designing a picture book with a friend who likes to write
* Drawing a chart of ideas
* Drawing a comic strip of an idea
* Drawing pictures of a story
* Doodling
* Exploring communication through various art forms and media
* Finding a picture related to content and describing it
* Guided visualizations
* Having the "big picture" first (an overview)
* Highlighting

* Looking at models
* Looking for pictures to represent concepts, or *picture association technique*
* Making a *Mind Map*
* Making time lines or graphs of action in a story
* Picturing what is to be said and listing descriptors to use in the telling
* Playing Pictionary
* Reading captions under pictures before reading the text
* Reading from charts, maps, and diagrams
* Reading while visualizing
* Seeing a map
* Seeing graphics
* Seeing objects or demonstrations
* Seeing pictures
* Seeing relationships visually portrayed
* Seeing textures
* Seeing the information on overheads/blackboards or white boards
* Underlining (with various colors)
* Using a camera or camcorder to record information
* Using a computer to do visual checking
* Using colored markers to highlight parts of words/sentences
* Using graphic organizers
* Using prepared note sheets (graphic organizers)
* Using visual imagery to practice reading or spelling by shape
* Using word processing with different colored letters

* Visualizing what is being said
* Watching a role-playing exercise
* Watching a video
* Writing down what is said

Picture Smart Reading Strategies

* Associate pictures with words or sounds
* Create personal bookmarks with visual reminders of words or letters
* Cut up colored acetate to lay over print to change figure-ground contrast
* Develop a word bank and post it when reading
* Find root words
* Focus on sight words
* Look for root words or word families
* Look for the same word or letter pattern in many different contexts, types of print, or media
* Look for the shape of words (short letters, tall letters, under-the-line letters)
* Make predictions based on pictures
* Pick out keywords
* Picture the word being stored in head
* See connections to previous learning
* Store words in a personal dictionary (notebook of alphabetized pages)
* Use color to highlight specific sounds
* Use colored flash cards
* Use finger, ruler, or pencil to keep place and point to letters, words, or sentences
* Use highlighter

* Use the *Fernald approach* for remembering new words
* Visually match word cards to text
* Write two similar words on a card and look for visual similarities and differences (e.g., want/went) and highlight differences

Picture Smart Writing Strategies

* Create a storyboard (boxes of visuals and keywords)
* Design the setting and costumes before writing a story
* Develop a *bubble map* for the key ideas before writing about them
* Develop a storyboard with the sequence and keywords
* Draw a picture of the ideas first, then describe them
* Edit with a visual exemplary model
* Highlight keywords
* Paint a picture to write about
* Photograph things to write about
* Use colored markers or overlays
* Use different shaped graphic organizers for each kind of writing
* Write from a concrete prop that is being described

Picture Smart Spelling Strategies

* Build the word out of tiles, felt letters, or plastic letters; jumble the order and rebuild
* Draw a picture embedding the shapes of the letters
* Find letter shapes in the environment
* Focus on the number of shapes in the word
* Identify tall letters, short letters, or letters above and below the line

* Remember the way the word looks
* Use colored letters or colored markers
* Use pipe cleaners to create shapes for letters
* Write the word in various colors or media

Picture Smart Math Strategies

* Associate a number to an object (e.g., 2 = a human, with two legs; 4 = a dog, with four legs)
* Color-code numbers
* Create a bar or line graph of the quantities
* Create *arrays*
* Design a picture book of math facts
* Do an interactive computer game with number facts (e.g., Concentration)
* Draw a picture to demonstrate the numbers and their relationships
* See quantities in head
* Substitute shapes for numbers (i.e., 3 = triangle)
* Use an abacus
* Watch a video on math concepts or facts
* Watch someone else do the problem, seeing it unfold
* Watch the numbers move and connect and change in the mind

Picture Smart Strategies to Pay Attention During a Lecture

* Color
* Doodle
* Draw cartoons
* Escape into the shapes of the room while still listening

* Focus on visual reinforcement
* Illustrate
* Look at people and read body language
* Look at props in room

* Look for patterns
* Take notes
* Watch for signs of body language from speaker

Picture Smart Note-Taking Strategies

* Create associative doodles
* Create pictures in the mind while listening
* Color-code notes
* Develop personal icons as abbreviations
* Learn shorthand symbols
* *Mind-Map* during direct teaching
* Obtain prepared note sheets
* See information on overheads or chalkboards
* Take notes in picture form
* Use *Cornell note-taking method*
* Use graphic organizers

Picture Smart Strategies When Frustrated

* Draw a picture of the feelings
* Identify the qualities of a peaceful environment and create them inside self
* Imagine how it feels to be calm
* Participate in art therapy
* Participate in *neuro-linguistic programming* (NLP)

* Relate feelings to a color or piece of artwork
* Use visual imagery to practice stress reduction
* Visualize a safe, peaceful place

Picture Smart Conflict-Resolution Strategies

* Choose colors that represent each phase of conflict resolution
* Create a flow chart of steps to resolve conflicts
* Create a storyboard of ways body language changes during the stages of conflict resolution
* Imagine a world free of conflicts
* Picture self in a setting that is free from stress, looking carefully at the setting and remembering details to recall during a conflict in order to relax
* See a video that discusses conflict resolution
* Videotape a conflict and then analyze what worked and what didn't
* Watch a conflict in a television program and then analyze it

Resources for the Picture Smart

* Advertisements
* Architecture programs
* Art catalogs
* Art classes
* Art institutes
* CD-ROMs
* Charts
* Children's museums

* Craft stores
* Graphic organizers
* Hobby centers
* Internet
* Maps
* Movies
* Photographs
* Pictures
* Postcards
* Storyboards
* Television shows
* Travel agencies
* Travel logs
* Videos

Body Smart:
The Bodily/Kinesthetic Intelligence

This person likes to:

* build;
* experience;
* feel and touch;
* make things;
* move.

Body Smart Scenario

Jason is active in class. He is a black belt in karate and he excels on the soccer field. He is fidgety in class but answers questions readily when called on. He has sloppy handwriting. His reading is slow, inaccurate, and a source of frustration for him. He slumps and withdraws when he has to do any task that requires memorization.

Body Smart Strategies Used

1. Jason starts using pipe cleaners in his hands during class. He rolls or twists them or builds small things that are relevant to the topics being discussed. They do not make noise and Jason knows that he needs to keep them within his personal space.

2. Jason starts to pace while reading or reviewing at home.

Results

Jason's activity level decreases in class. He is less disruptive. His pipe cleaner sculptures are often used by the teacher to review the concept that has been taught. For example, when the class is learning the concept of industrialization, Jason groups a bunch of small squares out of pipe cleaners, representing dense population and a factory. As a result of studying while moving, Jason's retention improves and so does his quiz and test performance.

Characteristics of the Body Smart Learner

* Active
* Athletic
* Does many, many things (acting, painting, sports)
* Dramatic
* Energetic
* Expresses competency through movement
* Is involved physically
* Learns best when concretely doing what is being taught
* Likes variety
* Makes things
* Thinks best when body is moving

Body Smart Strategies for Learning

The student who learns best through moving and feeling can use the following strategies:

* Body sculpting
* Choreographing
* Cooking

* Creating a board game of facts
* Creating art projects
* Cutting and pasting *sequence cards* of notes
* Dancing
* Dictation into a tape recorder while being driven or walking
* Doing a little at a time and taking "activity" breaks
* Doing experiments
* Doing hands-on or tactile activities
* Doing what is being learned
* Embodying
* Getting up and writing on the board
* Having something to squeeze or hold (e.g., Koosh ball, hand puzzle, Play-Doh)
* Internships
* Making an outline on large white board
* Miming
* Moving to different stations for different tasks
* Physically interpreting an understanding
* Playing charades
* Practicing many times
* Reading by moving book from side to side
* Rewarding self with physical activity or sport
* Role-playing
* Skipping, clapping, jumping, and hopping
* Taking field trips
* Taking notes on flash cards that can be reorganized
* Tapping toe inside of shoe so that no one can hear
* Using keyboard or typewriter

* Using sign language
* Walking and talking simultaneously
* Walking or exercising when thinking through information
* Walking or pacing while reading
* Writing a play and acting it out
* Writing ideas on index cards so ideas can be manipulated

Body Smart Reading Strategies

* Associate how the verbs would "feel" by thinking of the movement involved
* Connect each idea to a physical movement
* Feel each letter or word while saying it (*Fernald approach*, using crayon that is raised)
* Follow words with finger as someone else reads aloud
* Keyboard the letters
* Make body into letter shapes
* Make words out of Play-Doh, cardboard, felt, pipe cleaners, or other 3D objects
* Point to the word with finger, pointer, or pencil as you read
* Pretend to be the author
* Shuffle word cards and file in a meaningful way
* Think about the character's physical state
* Trace the word while reading it
* Use *Orton-Gillingham* or *Wilson* multisensory approaches
* Use Scrabble tiles or plastic letters

* Use word cards to build sentences
* Write in shaving cream (spread on desk and write, then erase)
* Write in the air or on a person's arm or back

Body Smart Writing Strategies

* Act out what you want to say before writing it down
* Build sentences out of plastic letters or word strips
* Develop ideas while exercising
* Edit by crossing out errors
* Learn specific physical movement of the pencil for each grapheme (*Lindamood* approach)
* Keyboard
* Write ideas on index cards or sticky notes and manipulate the order

Body Smart Spelling Strategies

* Build words out of objects: clay, plastic letters, Scrabble tiles, and felt boards
* Fernald approach
* Finger spell
* Move body into letter shapes
* Multisensory experience
* Repletion in building in different media
* Spell in sand
* Spread shaving cream on desk to write, then erase
* Use flash cards
* Use pipe cleaners to build words

Body Smart Math Strategies

* Act out the problems and solutions
* Build the problem with pipe cleaners or other objects
* Count on fingers
* Create a movement to represent each number
* Create word problems from life experiences

* Go on in-school field trips to locate number concepts (How many circles in the hall?)
* Have a different station in the room for different number concepts
* Learn sign language for numbers
* Move materials when counting (rods, abacus beads)
* Tap out the numbers
* Use manipulatives to solve problems
* Use parts of the body to represent different numbers
* Use plastic numbers
* Write numbers in clay

Body Smart Strategies to Pay Attention During a Lecture

* Ask questions
* Change posture
* Change or shift positions
* Chew gum
* Do isometrics
* Doodle
* Drink
* Eat
* Manipulate something that won't distract others
* Stretch

* Tap on leg
* Twiddle thumbs
* Yawn

Body Smart Note-Taking Strategies

* Keyboard
* Make something that represents what was heard
* Recopy notes
* Write while listening

Body Smart Strategies When Frustrated

* Bring a game or something to manipulate when work is complete
* Do a task that requires movement, such as mopping floors, punching tickets, being a hall monitor
* Exercise before required quiet time
* Go to the gym or outside for a few minutes before entering a structured situation
* Have a prop to juggle, hold, or squeeze
* Sit at the end of the table so that wiggling does not affect others

Body Smart Conflict-Resolution Strategies

* Become a balance (scale) and imagine putting the causes on one side and the effects on the other
* Focus on the body language of others
* Participate in *life space interviews*
* Role-play situations
* Think of a previous experience that was similar

Resources for the Body Smart

* Anything physical or movable
* Apprenticeships
* Athletics
* Body sculptures
* Building replicas
* Coaches
* Community activities
* Dance companies
* Explorers
* 4-H clubs
* Field trips
* Hands-on experiences
* Hikes
* Interactive museums
* Manipulatives
* Martial arts studios
* Physical movement
* Scouting
* *Shadowing*
* Sports analogies
* Sports figures

Self Smart:
The Intrapersonal Intelligence

This person likes to

* be alone;
* have time to think things through;
* reflect.

Self Smart Scenario

Roberto answers most questions directed to him with an "it depends" answer. He is able to come up with many different possibilities and gives his reasons for each one. Others describe him as "marching to the beat of a different drummer." Roberto seems knowledgeable, but it takes a long time for him to respond with specific information. On tests he is the last one to finish. His finished work shows thoughtfulness and time invested, but many assignments are not finished. He is inconsistent—sometimes motivated, other times lethargic and removed.

Self Smart Strategies Used

1. Roberto is given a list of topics and questions ahead of instruction, so that he can reflect on them and be prepared for what is coming.
2. Roberto starts keeping a diary of his thoughts and feelings.
3. Roberto is given extended time for classroom work and tests. When it is time to collect the papers, the

teacher quietly asks him to write on the top of the page how much additional time he needs and he is given this additional time later in the day.

Results

Roberto blossoms. Without time restrictions he is able to demonstrate what he knows. By having an appropriate and acceptable place to document his reflections, he can share his "decision" about the best answer without others hearing his process.

Characteristics of the Self Smart Learner

* Analytical
* Enjoys working alone
* Has few but close friends
* Independent
* Is a deep thinker
* Is self-aware
* Likes to go last
* Meditative
* Needs time to reflect
* Prefers to work in quiet
* Reflective

Self Smart Strategies for Learning

Students who learn best when pondering and reflecting can use the following strategies:

* Being given one word or task at a time; then allowed to sit in a quiet location and think, with no time limit and no interference by the tutor

* Brainstorming
* Discovering
* Drawing scenario
* Being given think time before responding
* Having freedom to be creative
* *Inquiry* method
* Integrating facts into a bigger whole
* Keeping a *diary*
* Listening to classical music or nature sounds in the background
* *Meditation*
* Musing
* Pondering
* Questioning
* Reading to self, not aloud
* Researching
* Reviewing
* Searching
* Studying
* Taking tests with extended time
* Theorizing
* Writing in a journal
* Writing summary of class activities

Self Smart Reading Strategies

* Analyze the process of reading
* Ask questions related to values, with no clear right or wrong answer

* Ask who would really need this information
* Be metacognitive
* Develop a personal word bank or dictionary
* Develop predictive questions prior to reading
* Develop questions to ask the tutor
* Focus on the overall meaning and not the decoding
* Identify the purpose of the reading
* Interpret the meaning of the passage in several ways
* Put word on one side of a card and the meaning or context on the other

* Read silently
* Reflect on the process ("Why is this a short *a* sound?")
* Self-correct materials using *assistive technology* (computer assisted learning or programmed text)
* Think about why the author wrote this
* Understand why words work the way they do
* Use *cloze passage* procedure to check on comprehension

Self Smart Writing Strategies

* Edit through self-reflection and error analysis
* Engage in *focused free writes*
* Have a model or examples to work from
* Journal privately
* Know in advance how the product will be judged
* Reflective writing
* Think time prior to writing

Self Smart Spelling Strategies

* Have a list of rules to which to refer to self-check
* Keep a list of words that have been problematic as a personal reference
* Use a spell checker or dictionary
* *Whole language* approach

Self Smart Math Strategies

* Creative associations for each number
* Discover the patterns of combining numbers
* Ponder one problem at a time
* Reason why numbers combine the way they do
* Research a formula
* Take time to think the problem through in a variety of ways

Self Smart Strategies to Pay Attention During a Lecture

* Agree/disagree
* Ask self questions ("How does this fit with what I believe?")
* Compare unknown/known
* Connect to personal values
* Daydream
* Draw on prior knowledge
* Project into future
* Reflect on previous information and connections
* Think of relevance
* When will this happen next

Self Smart Note-Taking Strategies

* Develop personal shorthand
* Focus on main thoughts, reflect on details later
* Relate information to personal experiences and feelings

Self Smart Strategies When Frustrated

* Develop a plan to prevent the incident from recurring
* Find the feelings that occur prior to the frustration
* Identify the feelings that led to the current situation and let them go
* Sit in a quiet location and think
* Visualize a change in behavior

Self Smart Conflict-Resolution Strategies

* Analyze what happened
* Develop a personal cause-and-effect chart
* Identify with feelings
* Reflect on the values expressed in the behavior
* Think of all possible consequences

Resources for the Self Smart

* Church-sponsored activities
* Cognitive therapy
* Dreams
* Eastern religions
* Individual psychotherapy
* Inspirational messages

* Meaningful pictures
* Meditation
* Native American writers
* Opportunities to be creative   .
* Philosophy
* Poetry
* Prayer
* Reflective music
* Religious orders
* Retreats
* Yoga
* Zen centers

Word Smart:
The Verbal/Linguistic Intelligence

This person likes to

* learn new vocabulary;
* play with words;
* read and write.

Word Smart Scenario

Rue loves learning vocabulary. He enthusiastically plays word games ("Think of a word that describes something that you see that starts with . . ."). Reading is pleasant and joyful. He makes up words that sound better than the original word ("gis-tusting" for *disgusting*). He easily memorizes lyrics to songs, even though he has trouble with melody. Writing quality and quantity are sometimes delayed because he's always looking for better word substitutions.

Word Smart Strategies Used

1. Rue is encouraged to use a thesaurus.
2. He creates a word bank as part of a brainstorming exercise before writing.
3. He uses a keyboard so that he can edit frequently, untroubled by erasures making holes in his paper.

Results

Rue expanded his speaking and writing vocabulary. He became a wordsmith for others, and became a writer for the school newspaper.

Characteristics of the Word Smart Learner

* Able to present orally or in writing
* Finds foreign languages easy to master
* Gets lost in reading
* Learns by hearing, reading, and writing
* Learns through language
* Likes to read
* Likes to talk
* Listens well to others
* Usually does well in traditional academic settings

Word Smart Strategies for Learning

The student who learns best through words can use the following strategies:

* Analyzing writing
* Being involved in reading-based group activities
* Describing information
* Dictating into a tape recorder
* Doing research projects
* Doing worksheets
* Editing others' writing
* Explaining information
* *Freewriting*

* Hearing information
* Keeping a diary
* Learning in the context of a story
* Outlining
* Reading abundant and varied materials
* Reading back something written
* Rereading notes
* Retelling stories
* Surfing the Internet
* Using a dictionary
* Using a thesaurus
* Using Cornell method
* Using mnemonics

* Using spell checkers, grammar checkers
* Writing creatively
* Writing dramatic scripts
* Writing journals
* Writing letters to friends describing what is being learned
* Writing or rewriting notes

Word Smart Reading Strategies

* Access the Internet
* Build vocabulary banks
* Carry a dictionary
* Copy words from the board
* Develop vocabulary
* Dictate stories

* Do crossword puzzles
* Find word families
* Learn a foreign language
* Learn prefixes, suffixes, and root words
* Master derivations
* Play Scrabble
* Pronounce the words aloud
* Read varied literature and genres
* Read aloud
* Read handouts with notes
* *Slot* for more descriptive words when editing
* Use a thesaurus
* Use phonics

Word Smart Writing Strategies

* Correspond with a pen pal
* Develop a vocabulary bank
* Discuss ideas
* Keep a diary
* Read a variety of authors and write paragraphs that model their styles
* Use whole language approach
* Write everything down

Word Smart Spelling Strategies

* Do word puzzles, crosswords, or Scrabble
* Find little words inside bigger words
* Find words in existing literature

* Increase vocabulary
* Keep a personal spelling log, writing down new words
* Learn derivations of words
* Master root words, suffixes, and prefixes
* Name the letters in a new word
* Put words into families
* Read more
* Read the word *martian* exactly the way it sounds (e.g., *friends* would be "fry ends")

Word Smart Math Strategies

* Connect number words to other words with the same roots
* Create story or word problems that require number facts
* Develop a mnemonic
* Explain to someone else the relationships of numbers
* Identify the sequence of events in a story
* Keep a math journal
* Learn to count or multiply in other languages
* Listen to someone explain numerical concepts
* Read about numbers and their constancies
* Read biographies of famous mathematicians
* Think of numbers as another language
* Treat numbers as a new vocabulary
* Write personal reactions to new ideas
* Write the steps to solving a problem in words

Word Smart Strategies to Pay Attention During a Lecture

* Attend to innuendo
* Create alphabet soup of personal abbreviations
* Follow along with handouts
* Listen for errors or contradictions
* Listen for new vocabulary or new use of vocabulary
* Listen for plays on words
* Read
* Read charts
* Take notes
* Translate buzzwords
* Use descriptive words

Word Smart Note-Taking Strategies

* Become class secretary
* Develop personal abbreviations
* Listen to recorded books and record key points
* Read other people's notes
* Rewrite scripts from television shows

Word Smart Strategies When Frustrated

* Read a book or article
* Talk into a tape recorder
* Tell what happened
* Write a journal or story

Word Smart Conflict-Resolution Strategies

* Describe feelings
* Develop a presentation about fighting to present to other classes
* Keep a diary of events and results
* Refer to *peer mediation*
* Respond to "What could you have done differently?"
* Talk it over with other combatant or into a tape recorder
* Tell the story
* Use life space interviews
* Write a composition about the incident and change the ending
* Write a letter to a parent, sibling, or friend describing what happened and the lesson learned

* Write the script (like a play) of who said what and in what order

Resources for the Word Smart

* Audiobooks
* Book clubs
* Classical literature
* Cloze passage
* Daily newspaper crossword puzzles
* Lecture series
* Public library
* Radio talk shows
* *Reader's Digest* Word Power quiz
* Story hour at libraries
* Unscramble letter games/puzzles
* Word searches
* Writer's guilds

Number Smart:
The Logical/Mathematical Intelligence

This person likes to

* be precise;
* figure out relationships;
* have a special goal;
* know how to solve things.

Number Smart Scenario

David quickly remembers phone numbers. His mother can always count on him to remember phone numbers she needs to know. His highest grades are in math. As a reluctant reader, he stops doing most of his homework. Spelling is his poorest subject—he never receives more than 50 percent on any spelling test during the year.

Number Smart Strategies Used

1. David automatically turns letters into their numerical position in the alphabet (C = 3, I = 9).
2. David makes a number/letter line and posts it on his desk.
3. David develops a formula for spelling words like phone numbers ("helipad" converted to 8-5-12-9-16-1-4).

Results

David's performance on weekly spelling tests improves to 85 percent for the remainder of the year. He starts raising his hand in reading group to volunteer to read. He attempts a higher percentage of homework assignments.

Characteristics of the Number Smart Learner

* Analytical
* Applies math well
* Bottom-line person
* Comfortable with numbers
* Concrete
* Efficient
* Goal-oriented
* Likes comparisons
* Logical
* Measures progress
* Methodical
* Money manager
* Organized
* Practical
* Precise
* Sequential
* Simplifies things
* Thinks in steps and sequences

Number Smart Strategies for Learning

The student who learns best with sequence, structure, and organization can use these strategies:

* Brainstorming ideas and then sequencing them in order
* Calculating
* Categorizing
* Collecting data on the frequency of a word or combination of letters
* Concluding
* Creating a time line
* Developing a chart of choices and consequences
* Developing a problem map or flow chart
* Developing a system of organization
* Developing an action plan
* Diagramming the steps to a problem and the encounter
* Dividing lessons into parts
* Following a pattern or formula
* Having a worksheet to practice working out problems
* Having an agenda and a "to do" list
* Having orderly assignments
* Learning step by step
* Making outlines or lists
* *Matrix*
* Organizing work space
* Preplanning and preparing
* Scheduling
* Seeing patterns

* Seeking information to accomplish goals
* Setting up a timeline for accomplishing tasks
* Setting structure and clearly defined goals
* Thinking of ways to simplify process
* Using charts with questions to structure thoughts
* Using math applications
* Using numbers as memory triggers
* Writing a checklist for what needs to be accomplished
* Writing out steps of a process

Number Smart Reading Strategies

* Alphabetize new words
* Analyze errors and find patterns
* Be aware of length of assignment (how many pages)
* Categorize words by characteristics in the words (e.g., phonemes, consonants, vowels)

* Count number of words in a sentence with similar sounds
* Create "to do" list
* Develop a sheet with the rules and exceptions
* Develop checklist of personal strategies for how to attack words
* Estimate the amount of time needed to complete the assignment
* Have a way to check own answers (e.g., programmed text, answer key)
* Keep records of progress
* Learn rules for sounds, word patterns, suffixes, and prefixes

* Look for patterns
* Master *Glass analysis* of word clusters
* Organize the directions
* Put cards in order
* Read the summary prior to the entire passage
* Sort words or sounds by likes and differences
* Understand the rules for grammar
* Use *five W's and H*
* Use word families
* Use word lists

Number Smart Writing Strategies

* Analyze errors
* Brainstorm ideas and then sequence them by number
* Categorize information that should be grouped
* Chart progress
* Compare own writing to a model or rubric
* Have traditional outline
* Know how long it needs to be
* List the rules for editing
* Sequence ideas prior to writing
* Think about the main point and supporting detail
* Use a formula for necessary elements (topic sentence and three details)
* Use charts with questions
* Work out a logical progression to explain the information

Number Smart Spelling Strategies

* Analyze options
* Check the rule of the word's pattern
* Convert letters to numbers (A = 1, B = 2, C = 3, etc.)
* Develop a systematic approach for mastery
* Find clues for exceptions
* Group words into families, clusters, or phonemes
* Have a master list of rules to use as a resource
* Know the number of patterns possible (e.g., six major types of words)
* Learn spelling rules and exceptions
* Master other languages to learn derivations

Number Smart Math Strategies

* Build on the steps or progressions
* Explore hundreds grids to find patterns
* Figure out the similarities and differences
* Have a logical sequence
* Identify formulas
* Make a number grid
* Use money

Number Smart Strategies to Pay Attention During a Lecture

* Calculate
* Categorize
* Chart

* Check off agenda
* Count number of times speaker says "uh"
* Create formula
* Extrapolate the key words
* Identify the logic or other structure
* Label
* List tasks for later
* Outline
* Watch clock

Number Smart Note-Taking Strategies

* Have examples for each concept
* Identify key words
* Integrate lecture notes with book notes
* Organize information
* Take notes in structured formats
* Use Cornell method of note taking
* Weigh the important against the unessential

Number Smart Strategies When Frustrated

* Count to 10
* Diagram the steps to the problem
* Do math problems or Sudoku while calming down
* Keep a log of events and relate what may be causing them
* Make a list of feelings and incidents, and create a time line

Number Smart Conflict-Resolution Strategies

* Analyze the reasons for both sides
* Collect data on incidents
* Develop a chart of choice-consequences
* Develop a process for resolution
* Develop an action plan
* Learn the court system
* Review the peer mediation process

Resources for the Number Smart

* Accountants
* Banks
* Bus schedules
* Business plans
* Calendars
* Checkbooks
* DOS-based computers
* Legends on maps
* Managers
* Menus
* Recipes
* Science organizations
* Time lines

Nature Smart:
The Naturalist Intelligence

This person likes to

* categorize;

* collect;

* grow;

* plant;

* relate to animals;

* sort.

Nature Smart Scenario

By kindergarten, Billy knows everything there is to know about dinosaurs. He doesn't know how he learned it all, and neither does his mother. He instinctually has a sense about animals as well. He knows the eating and sleeping habits of many creatures that live in the woods near his home. In class he is often bored, insensitive to the needs of other students, and impatient when they need repetition to learn something that he already knows. As the school year evolves, Billy is either attacking others or hibernating in his own corner of the room.

Nature Smart Strategies Used

1. Billy is encouraged to draw parallels between situations in class and the natural world. For example, when discussing his impulsivity, he learns to pretend he is an eagle, soaring above and watching carefully for his dinner, only then swooping down at the last minute so as not to scare his prey away.

2. Billy's teacher asks him for an analogy from nature for every concept she teaches. For example, when doing a unit on neighbors, Billy is asked to think of ways in which animals demonstrate being "neighborly."

Results

Billy grows to accept his need to be in harmony with his school environment. He develops patience and understanding. He migrates to an older classroom for science. He tabulates his need for hibernation time and develops a cycle for it, monitoring his own needs and evolving into a more efficient student.

Characteristics of the Nature Smart Learner

* Aware of changes in weather or growing patterns
* Enjoys collecting natural phenomena (e.g., rocks, leaves)
* Environmentalist
* Expert in some species or natural substance
* Learns best when relating new information to something in nature
* Likes to garden or farm or train or rehab animals
* Sensitive to animals

Nature Smart Strategies for Learning

The learner who thinks best using natural phenomena could use the following strategies:

* Being aware of environmental impact
* Collecting
* Connecting a natural phenomenon that parallels new content being learned
* Developing collections (e.g., rocks, leaves)
* Exploring the woods, rivers, and oceans
* Finding patterns in natural objects
* Spending time in nature
* Taking field trips to natural resources
* Thinking up experiments

Nature Smart Reading Strategies

* Associate each letter symbol with an animal or plant (Z = zebra)
* Categorize words by where they fit in nature (animal, vegetable, or mineral)
* Connect each letter sound to a sound from nature (bird call)
* Create same/different charts of letters or sounds
* Read about natural phenomena
* Read weather reports in daily paper or on Internet
* Sequence story events, such as the stages of growth of a favorite species
* Sort letters of the alphabet by shape, color, or length
* Watch the Discovery, Animal Planet, or Weather channels on television

Nature Smart Writing Strategies

* Ask how nature records meaningful things
* Image how you would feel about a topic if you were a bird, a fish, or a volcano
* Relate the writing to the communication style of your favorite animal
* Think about how the earth writes on us
* Write a story about the adventures of a leaf that landed in the ocean: what might happen to it, and where it might travel

Nature Smart Spelling Strategies

* Find patterns of detailed shapes in nature (e.g., veins on leaves are all different)
* Learn how to spell words from nature
* Manipulate natural objects to make words
* Practice spelling with clay, sand, gravel, or water

Nature Smart Math Strategies

* Associate numbers to the natural world
* Count the days of the month by watching the moon
* Count types of rocks/animals/plants in a collection
* Do a leaf collection and tabulate types and quantities
* Identify growing seasons and their length
* Listen to or watch the weather forecast and analyze how the numbers are used
* Tabulate days of sunshine
* Watch for numerical patterns in nature (flocks, herds, dens)

Nature Smart Strategies to Pay Attention During a Lecture

* Attend to the breeze on your face
* Put self elsewhere
* Stare out window
* Tune in to the environment (e.g., temperature, weather, campfire)

Nature Smart Note-Taking Strategies

* Compare animal tracks to notes
* Take notes using different materials (paper, ink, wax)

Nature Smart Strategies When Frustrated

* Decide how nature handles frustration
* Learn about biorhythms
* Listen to CDs or tapes of nature sounds
* Ponder the natural flow of the environment
* Reflect on how certain animals respond to frustration
* Spend time in woods or next to flowing water

Nature Smart Conflict-Resolution Strategies

* Analyze the life cycle of certain plants and animals
* Create cause-and-effect charts of animals or fish
* Learn how nature responds to conflict

Resources for the Nature Smart

* Bird-watchers
* Coast Guard
* Conservationists
* Environmentalists
* Farmers
* Forest rangers
* Greenpeace
* Hiking clubs
* Landscapers
* National parks
* Natural resources departments
* Parks departments
* Sailing or boating clubs
* Watch the Discovery, Animal Planet, or Weather channels
* Water departments
* Weather stations
* Zoos

People Smart:
The Interpersonal Intelligence

This person likes to

* be with people;
* empathize;
* interact;
* lead;
* teach.

People Smart Scenario

Ashley spends much of her day talking with others. She interacts with everyone, whenever possible. She volunteers to help the teacher, asks her friends whether they need help, or just chats. Ashley has a winning smile and loves to give hugs. She cannot do the board work in class and is no longer willing to read in front of others. She does not do assignments, and work brought home isn't brought back to school.

People Smart Strategies Used

1. Ashley identifies reading as her biggest concern. She and her teacher pick out two words she wants to master: Toronto and Florida.

2. Ashley is asked to identify names of people inside of the words she wants to learn. She finds *Ron, Flo*, and *Ida*. She uses these clues to retain these words.

3. Ashley is "hired" as an aide in a multiage special-education classroom for one hour a day to teach one child at a time one letter sound per week.

Results

Ashley chooses the letter C to start. On the day she is supposed to start her "job," she brings in a shoebox full of toys, junk, trinkets, and pictures. She spent hours collecting things she can use to help her new student learn the sound that C makes. She is very successful with student number 1, and then moves on to student number 2. Ashley spends an hour a day in that classroom helping others. She learns all the sounds she teaches.

Characteristics of the People Smart Learner

* Active group member
* Charismatic
* Compromising
* Descriptive
* Enjoys working with people
* Friendly
* Giving
* Good communicator
* Likes to learn in groups
* Listens
* Nurturing
* Outgoing
* Perceptive
* Persuasive

* Sensitive to others' needs
* Strong leader
* Remembers characters from books or films
* Remembers stories about people
* Takes risks
* Talkative
* Thinks aloud
* Values relationships
* Wants feedback

People Smart Strategies for Learning

The student who learns best by working with others can use the following strategies:

* Acting out what is learned
* Asking peers for ideas
* Asking questions
* Being validated
* Brainstorming with others
* Connecting to the teacher
* *Contracting for learning* with another person
* Creating support network
* Debating
* Dictating
* Discussing
* Group work
* Having show-and-tell
* Hiring personal tutor or coach
* Imagining being in others' shoes
* Interviewing

* Learning information through others' experiences
* Listening
* Participating in community service projects
* Role-playing situations
* Staying after class to work with the teacher
* Teaching someone else
* Telephone appointments
* Using tape recorder
* Working with a buddy
* Writing to a friend

People Smart Reading Strategies

* Associate sounds to individuals
* Develop lists of adjectives that describe people
* Join a book club
* Listen to a sound recording
* Listen to others read aloud
* Predict characters' actions
* Read biographies
* Read plays
* Read works written in dialect
* Reciprocal teaching

* Retell
* Take oral quizzes
* Talk aloud
* Teach
* Think about the author's point of view
* Tutor peers

* Write letters
* Write personal experiences, making them into a book to share

People Smart Writing Strategies

* Create scripts for advertising
* Develop list of adjectives to describe people
* Grade others' writing, using predetermined matrix
* Listen to others read their writing
* Participate in *group writes*
* Proofread others' work
* Use authentic language
* Write in dialect
* Write letters
* Write plays or scripts

People Smart Spelling Strategies

* Cooperative learning
* Find people's names inside words
* Match personal invented spelling with someone else's
* Reciprocal teaching
* Work with a tutor or a study buddy

People Smart Math Strategies

* Ask questions
* Associate difficult facts with personal acquaintances
* Discuss reasons or observations
* Interview others on how they solved the problem

* Learn through others' mistakes
* Share ideas with others
* Talk about personal math discoveries
* Teach someone else

People Smart Strategies to Pay Attention During a Lecture

* Argue
* Ask side questions
* Comment to a friend
* Decide whom you will sit with
* Discuss
* Dominate
* Facilitate movements
* Humor
* Interact with presenter
* Joke
* Judge
* Listen for nonverbal communication from the speaker
* Nonverbal interaction
* Observe others
* Sarcasm
* Tease

People Smart Note-Taking Strategies

* Compare notes with another student
* Have someone else take notes while talking or participating
* Rewrite for a younger child (by making language simpler)

* Share and review notes with a friend
* Take notes for someone who is absent
* Think about what the author thought was important
* Use someone else's notes as a model

People Smart Strategies When Frustrated

* Give permission to call home
* Develop personal relationship with the student
* Have a pass or a signal that allows student to remove self from the situation
* Imagine how someone else would feel
* Invite a friend to call
* Read story about a person with a similar problem, and talk it out

People Smart Conflict-Resolution Strategies

* Attend *scared straight* presentation
* Become involved in group therapy
* Contract for learning with another person who is respected
* Create a *circle of friends* to provide feedback
* Imagine being "in another person's shoes"
* Interview someone who has been in trouble with the law
* Meet with a counselor
* Participate in peer mediation or peer court
* Relate to an incident on a television sitcom
* Role-play situation
* Shadow a person who is good at avoiding conflict

Resources for the People Smart

* Babysitting
* *Bibliotherapy*
* Chat rooms
* Clubs
* Community service
* Dialogues
* Hospital candy stripers
* Interviews
* Plays
* Reading biographies
* Relating to characters
* Shadowing others
* Volunteer organizations
* Watching biographies on television

3

STRENGTH-BASED
INTERVENTIONS

Teachers have found a variety of ways to use the theory of Multiple Intelligences in academic settings. This chapter includes examples of strength-based interventions compiled from classroom teachers around the country. For each topic or scenario you will find several ideas for each Smart Part. Use them as a basis for building your own strategy banks for these typical classroom experiences. They should provide you with ideas that you can easily translate into whatever you are teaching, through each intelligence.

The following pages will provide you with a quick reference for differentiating learning in a wide variety of topics. Each entry contains a list reflecting all eight intelligences—the Smart Parts—and methods by which you can tap each intelligence for the specific skill or behavior.

These MI intervention plans have been divided into three major categories:

Behavior, Discipline, and Motivation
    Cause and Effect
    Discipline
    Prevention
    Getting Along with Others

Change

Stress Reduction

Learning Patience

Self-Advocacy

Taking Responsibility

Task Completion

Time Management

Writing Down Assignments

Dealing with Boredom

The Learning Process

Getting Ready for Homework

Making Memory Mindful

Trying to Remember Specific Information

Organizing a Desk

Remembering Chores

Word Problems

Learning Vocabulary

Decoding Words

Reading Comprehension

Visualization Skills

Assessment

An Example

Rubric

Tic-Tac-Do

Evaluation Grid

Behavior, Discipline, and Motivation

Behavior management is a major issue in today's schools. Students are acting out in ways that upset teachers, administrators, peers, and even the students who are acting out.

Look at a typical student who is referred to the office. "Sam" is often physically inappropriate. He creates distractions in class by making clicking noises or tapping his feet or fingers on the desk. The teacher tries to distract him, but Sam's attention span is very short. Sam's reading skills are weak, but his biggest problem seems to be his inability to sit still and listen.

So what typically happens? Sam is punished by being made to sit still in another location, where he won't distract others. But does he sit still in the new location? If you watch, his fidgety behavior will likely continue . . . and this elicits another lecture. Listening to directions has not been an effective learning strategy for Sam.

What can you do differently?

If your purpose for doing behavior management is to *teach* students more appropriate behavior, then you need to design intervention strategies that tap into each student's strengths, and find ways to help the student evaluate how well learning is happening. Howard Gardner's MI model can help you to rethink strategies that might be "brain friendly" for Sam or any student. Five strength-based intervention scenarios follow.

Cause and Effect

For students to learn appropriate behavior, they need to learn how to predict the consequences of their behavior. This can be learned through all the intelligences.

To Better Understand Cause and Effect,
Students Who Are Music Smart Can:

* write and perform a rap
* find songs that have fighting or conflict resolution as a theme
* design an orchestra where the members fight
* see "patterns" of behavior and translate them into patterns in music
* write music that demonstrates feelings and the peaceful resolution

Picture Smart Students Can:

* develop a storyboard of the conflict cycle
* create a graphic organizer or flow chart showing the elements that lead to conflict
* watch a movie about a conflict and analyze the patterns of behavior
* develop a chart of behaviors that work to solve problems
* collect cartoons that show conflict resolution

Students Who Are Body Smart Can:

* think through the rules in a favorite sport
* relate the conflict to an athletic event
* build a replica of the conflict
* create a game that would involve the steps taken in conflict resolution
* role-play the steps leading to conflict
* identify the movements that precipitate conflict and compare them to the body movements that encourage cooperation

Self Smart Students Can:

*   spend quiet time reflecting on what happened and their personal role in the events
*   do a time-out
*   identify their personal feelings about the incident
*   reflect on what could have been different
*   record (in words, pictures, music, or 3-D) the feelings that led up to the incident as well as the feelings that have resulted from the incident
*   develop a personal mantra as a reminder of what should be done
*   create a personal contract complete with goal setting and personal choices

Word Smart Students Can:

*   do *journaling* or describe the scenario
*   listen to someone who has been in a similar conflict
*   hear the other person's story on tape
*   write a script (for a play) of who said what and in what order
*   respond to the question "What could you have done differently?"
*   write a composition about the incident and change the ending
*   develop a presentation for other classes about fighting
*   write a letter to the parent describing what happened, how it happened, and the lesson learned

Students Who Are Number Smart Can:

*   develop a process for resolution (a problem map or a flow chart)

* collect data on incidents or problems in the lunchroom
* develop a chart of choices and consequences
* review a peer mediation process
* analyze the reasons for both participants' actions
* develop an action plan

Students Who Are Nature Smart Can:

* relate the conflict to a conflict in nature
* research how feelings are resolved in the animal kingdom
* watch a documentary on animals and/or plants and analyze the cause and effect described
* develop a cause-and-effect flow chart of what supports positive growth in nature
* do scientific experiments designed to collect data on the effects of different environmental conditions (sunshine, weather, nutrients, etc.) on organisms

People Smart Students Can:

* meet with a mediator or attend peer mediation
* shadow a person who is good at avoiding conflict
* role-play the situation, including the participants' feelings
* relate to something seen on a television sitcom
* invite parents to a "sharing"
* create a circle of friends to provide feedback
* imagine being "in the other person's shoes"
* attend a "scared straight" presentation
* interview someone who has been in trouble with the law because of fighting

Discipline

Teachers want their students to learn from discipline, and to take responsibility for their actions. Interventions for discipline can be reinforced by each of the intelligences:

To Better Appreciate a Disciplinary Action,
Students Who Are Music Smart Can:

* think of a song that reminds them of how to behave
* identify a rhythm signal to know when a behavior issue is escalating

Picture Smart Students Can:

* draw what happened that caused them to get into trouble
* do a storyboard of the event that resulted in the discipline, but change the last picture to make a more positive outcome
* think of a movie scene that shows a better choice

Body Smart Students Can:

* act out or role-play
* make a model representing _____
* make an analogy to how penalties are called and enforced in football or some other sport

Self Smart Students Can:

* think about what was done
* reflect on the feelings it aroused
* ask, "Would this behavior ever be considered appropriate? When? Where?"
* reflect, "Were you asking yourself 'deep questions' about consequences?"

Word Smart Students Can:

* talk it out

* do life space interviews with an adult

* use bibliotherapy: ask others for names of people or books that the learner would enjoy and that would reinforce appropriate behavior

Number Smart Students Can:

* keep a tally or personal rating scale on effective behavior

* analyze personal behavior to find patterns, thereby creating rules that show the consequences

Nature Smart Students Can:

* think of metaphors in nature

* tend to a plant or animal in a caring way

* ask, "What would happen if birds _____?"

People Smart Students Can:

* tell someone what happened and ask for feedback

* think of famous fictional characters who could be used as role models

* think about how someone else would feel in this situation

Prevention

Here are strategies to help students to learn self-discipline and to prevent inappropriate behavior.

Music Smart Students Can:

* write raps about fighting and violence
* find jobs in the school related to music
* do a music inventory of the school
* research the kind of music that calms people down
* connect with a musical advocate or mentor
* be rewarded with music for good behavior
* be featured in a talent show

Picture Smart Students Can:

* draw pictures
* visualize a quiet, conflict-free place
* think of a color that is calming
* look at a painting that is calming
* paint
* do a puzzle
* create a visual metaphor for conflict resolution

Body Smart Students Can:

* use a Koosh ball, worry stone, or other nonviolent object
* pace
* learn to move without being a distraction to others
* pay attention to personal breathing
* focus on the physical location (in the body) of anger or frustration (i.e., stomach, hands, throat, etc.)
* build a personal "fort" that is safe from conflict

Self Smart Students Can:

* sit in a quiet location and think—with no time limit
* develop a plan to prevent the incident from recurring
* visualize a change in behavior

Word Smart Students Can:

* write a journal or story
* talk into a tape recorder whenever upset
* read a book or article

Number Smart Students Can:

* do math problems, puzzles, or mazes to calm down
* make a list of feelings or incidents, or a time line of events
* diagram the steps of the problem

Nature Smart Students Can:

* imagine what the "wise owl" would do
* create a space in the building which simulates a calming, "natural" environment

People Smart Students Can:

* have a "pass" or a signal allowing access to help
* call home or call someone special (lifeline)

Getting Along with Others

Sometimes students have to work with someone they don't particularly like. Here are some things learners can do to get along with more people more of the time.

Music Smart Students Can:

* think of songs about getting along with people or feeling good about people:
  ✓ "Lean on Me" (Bill Withers, *Still Bill*, 1972)
  ✓ "People" (Barbra Streisand, *People*, 1964)
  ✓ "Won't You Be My Neighbor?" (Fred M. Rogers, *Mister Rogers' Neighborhood*, 1967)

Picture Smart Students Can:

* watch a movie about how to get along, and think about what the characters did to make it work; for example, in *Ice Age* (Wedge & Saldanha, 2002) two enemies learn how to work together and help each other

Body Smart Students Can:

* ask themselves, "How do people show other people that they like them or are happy for them, just using their bodies?" and see how many physical actions they can come up with (smiling, clapping, shaking hands, etc.)

Self Smart Students Can:

* think of times when other people have shown that they liked or cared about them. What did they do? How did other people's actions make them feel good? Can they do some of the same things?

Word Smart Students Can:

    ✻   think of stories or books read where the characters took care of each other. How did Peter Pan and Wendy take care of the boys? How did Tinker Bell help? What about the Seven Dwarfs? They were different from one another, but how did they get along?

Number Smart Students Can:

    ✻   think about the Golden Rule: How can they use this "formula" to change personal behavior?

Nature Smart Students Can:

    ✻   observe an ant colony, where each ant has a job and they work well together. Ask, "What other animals or insects are good at getting along with others? How do they do it?"

People Smart Students Can:

    ✻   think of someone who is good at helping others and ponder what that person does to show care. Some examples might be:

    ✓ Mister Rogers

    ✓ a librarian

    ✓ a friendly aide

Change

Change is something students will have to deal with throughout their lives. There are many different ways for them to deal with change, depending on their Smart Parts.

Music Smart Students Can:

* ask, "How will it sound when I change one instrument in a piece? Will it affect the rest of the piece? Which part would I want to change first, the main theme or variation, or the supporting instruments?"

Picture Smart Students Can:

* ask, "What will this look like if I change it? How can I help others understand my vision? How will change shape the 'big picture'? How can I see this from several points of view?"

Body Smart Students Can:

* ask, "What materials do I need to make this happen?" and then "roll up their sleeves" and get to work

Self Smart Students Can:

* contemplate the outcome before acting, thinking, "I need some time to ponder this. It reminds me of when I _____. Change elicits many different feelings in me. I wonder if it will be positive or negative? It could be both."

Word Smart Students Can:

* ask, "Can I define this change? Is there research to support it? Who has written about the topic of change? Many novels deal with how the main

character changes. That change is often based on conflict or is a reaction to a crisis. What book do I think of as a model for change?"

Number Smart Students Can:

* think, "Let me plan this out carefully and logically. How much will it cost? I should research, identify the goals, list the objectives, and create a time line and make sure I can measure improvement."

Nature Smart Students Can:

* ask, "How will this change affect the environment? What analogy can I think of in nature? In the larger picture of the world, where does this fit? I'd like to observe the natural phenomenon, try some pilot groups, and then collect data on the change."

People Smart Students Can:

* reflect, "Whom can I work with on this? How will the other people feel? Is it in the best interest of those who participate? How can I help others to cope with the impact of the change? I look forward to the new people who I can serve if this happens. I really admire _____ because of the way he (or she) demonstrated a positive way to make the most of change."

Stress Reduction

We all sometimes feel stressed. When students feel this way, they have choices about what to do to decrease their level of anxiety. Here are a few strategies.

Music Smart Students Can:

* play music or nature sounds that are from 30 to 60 beats per minute, simulating resting heart rate

Picture Smart Students Can:

* draw or paint, focusing on a space that is restful and soothing

Body Smart Students Can:

* work out, play a high-energy game (e.g., racquetball), or go for a run

Self Smart Students Can:

* take some quiet time, curl up in a relaxed setting with a favorite book or a pad of paper to sketch in, or write poetry

Word Smart Students Can:

* write down their thoughts
* write a letter to the person or situation that is causing the stress; don't mail it, but put it away for a reread later

Number Smart Students Can:

* think about the cause of the stress; identify alternative paths and their consequences

Nature Smart Students Can:

* go for a walk in the woods, spend time with a pet, go horseback riding, or walk on the beach

People Smart Students Can:

* call a friend who is a good listener

Learning Patience

Sometimes it is hard to wait for other people to finish their work or ready themselves for the next activity. Here are some things a student can do to learn patience.

Music Smart Students Can:

* sing a song in their heads

Picture Smart Students Can:

* visualize or replay a movie in their heads

Body Smart Students Can:

* do movements that won't bother other people ("moving without disturbing" strategies)

Self Smart Students Can:

* daydream about anything

Word Smart Students Can:

* read a book or write in a journal or diary

Number Smart Students Can:

* estimate the mean waiting time in hours, minutes, and seconds, then compare the actual mean waiting time to the time yesterday or the day before

Nature Smart Students Can:

  * imagine being in a favorite place and relive the smells, sounds, and other physical properties of that place

People Smart Students Can:

  * think of ways to help others complete their work successfully

Self-Advocacy

When students learn differently, it is important for them to let others know what works for them. Here are some ways for students to do this.

Music Smart Students Can:

  * practice self-advocacy by tape-recording the words they would use. They could then relisten for voice tone; is it one of confidence, yet politeness and respect? How did the request sound? Did they hear a voice that made them want to listen and answer yes?

Picture Smart Students Can:

  * visualize themselves getting exactly what is needed, whether it be an alternative assignment or a test mod, that would allow them to bypass the weakness but still show knowledge
  * look at the environment, the colors, and the textures that would allow for greatest success; create a graphic organizer to reproduce this experience

Body Smart Students Can:

  * ask, "How does my body feel when I self-advocate and get what I need? How do I sit? What about my eye contact? Where do I position myself? How close do I stand to the person with whom I'm communicating?"

* practice the language of self-advocacy by doing it with people they already trust, then with people with whom they have less of a relationship

Self Smart Students Can:

* think, "You can control your own destiny as long as you stay focused on what you know works best for you. Think about yourself, your strengths, your weaknesses, and what strategies and environment you need to compensate for them. Remember, no one knows your brain better than you do, so make sure you stay in touch with what you know will work."

Word Smart Students Can:

* plan and write the script to use when self-advocating, making sure to use words that are assertive (neither passive nor aggressive)
* think of books read in which characters were good self-advocates, then use words from these characters to help compose dialogue

Number Smart Students Can:

* create a chart or checklist of the things to include when self-advocating; include strengths and weaknesses; use cognitive strengths to compensate for weaknesses
* think of the logic of personal requests, and come up with several alternatives or modifications

Nature Smart Students Can:

* collect data on the strategies used when doing things "naturally" (such as a favorite hobby); apply these data to the school "environment"

People Smart Students Can:

* practice advocacy skills with family members; tell them ahead of time what they will be doing, and ask them to comment specifically on how effective the self-advocacy was

Taking Responsibility

Taking responsibility means taking care of oneself. It is important for students to learn strategies that will allow them to be independent and responsible for their own behaviors.

Music Smart Students Can:

* make up a song about being responsible and sing it quietly

Picture Smart Students Can:

* give themselves a visual reward, drawing a "prize" for being responsible

Body Smart Students Can:

* link responsible behavior to a typical physical movement (such as tapping a finger). Then, whenever they do that movement, it should trigger a reminder to be responsible

Self Smart Students Can:

* create a personal goal and link it to a feeling

Word Smart Students Can:

* read self-help books

Number Smart Students Can:

* write a contract with themselves, with steps, goals, and rewards

* log successes and failures

Nature Smart Students Can:

* observe responsible behavior in nature and emulate the pattern

People Smart Students Can:

* interview some admired person who is responsible

Task Completion

It is important for students to finish what they start. Here are some ideas for a student who tends to put things off, or to start things and not finish them.

Music Smart Students Can:

* play a favorite song in their heads while doing the task, or do the task to the rhythm of the song

Picture Smart Students Can:

* use a small, colored egg timer to monitor how much time is left to complete the task, noting how much sand has moved from the top to the bottom

Body Smart Students Can:

* use a vibrating watch, the type used by people who are hearing impaired; have the vibrator signal when the time is almost elapsed

Self Smart Students Can:

* prepare for the task by reflecting on ideas ahead of time, creating a plan for how to accomplish it

Word Smart Students Can:

* create a poem or a first-letter mnemonic with key words to recall what is needed in order to complete the task in a timely way

Number Smart Students Can:

* break down the entire task into minitasks, then predict how long each minitask will take; check each one off after completion

Nature Smart Students Can:

* think of how the seasons change in spite of what may be happening in people's lives—the clock, too, keeps ticking (How do animals and plants meet the deadlines of the seasons?)

People Smart Students Can:

* "contract" with someone else to remind them how much time is left to complete a task
* look at the body language of other people to determine how much time is left

Time Management

Students need to be able to finish things on time. They may even need reminders of how long something will take, or how much time is left before the work must be submitted. Here are some ideas that will help students know how much time is left in a task.

Music Smart Students Can:

* play a song in their heads; when it is "done," they should be finished as well

Picture Smart Students Can:

* create clocks with icons of what needs to be done when the hands are in a certain place
* have specific locations or spaces for different tasks

Body Smart Students Can:

* use a clock or phone timer with vibration

Self Smart Students Can:

* think of personal connections to the amount of time that is left
* think of how being late would feel

Word Smart Students Can:

* write a page in a diary every day, and time it to see how long it takes

Number Smart Students Can:

* use a timer to indicate how much time is left
* write out steps, an agenda, or goals with a time estimate for completing each one

Nature Smart Students Can:

* think of an animal that is always on time, and create a personal analogy

People Smart Students Can:

* ask someone to call at a set time to warn the student there is two minutes remaining

Writing Down Assignments

For students to get their work done, they must write down the assignment properly, or else by the time they get home they won't remember what the teacher requested. Here are a few solutions to the problem.

Music Smart Students Can:

* listen to the rhythm of the teacher's voice; how does the teacher's voice change when giving an assignment? Listen for this tonal "clue"

Picture Smart Students Can:

* carry colored pencils or crayons, one designated for each day of the week
* draw a cartoon character to act as an assignment monitor; make up stickers with the character's picture to be put in notebook whenever there is an assignment

Body Smart Students Can:

* move stickers from a pad to an assignment folder daily
* go up to the assignment board to double-check that everything has been recorded

* check assignment pad (always placed in the same location in book bag or pocket) before leaving class

Self Smart Students Can:

* think of the sense of pride that they will feel when every assignment is jotted down without anyone else nagging or reminding

Word Smart Students Can:

* make up a new word story that can be used to remember writing down assignments

Number Smart Students Can:

* think about the classroom schedule—what time does each subject start and stop? When does the teacher usually write down the assignments? Set up a routine to write them down each day

Nature Smart Students Can:

* observe the typical amount of light outside when writing down assignments. Is it early morning? Are there long shadows or short ones outside the classroom window? Match the task to the sun's movement

People Smart Students Can:

* volunteer to be the person in class who tells people who were absent what the previous day's assignments were

Dealing with Boredom

For students whose minds wander when they are supposed to be doing something else, here are a few ideas to get their brains reinvolved.

Music Smart Students Can:

* think of a song that reminds them of what is supposed to be done; play it in their heads loudly, then softly. Which sounds better? How can one improve the sound, but still connect it to the thing he or she is supposed to be doing?

Picture Smart Students Can:

* convert a task to a mental cartoon, morphing the characters from the present, then play the cartoon fast or slow

Body Smart Students Can:

* convert a task to a physical action or a sport
* take out quiet manipulatives, such as Play-Doh or chenille sticks, and build quietly; make the building relate to the topic

Self Smart Students Can:

* escape to a "private place" to think about what makes it different from the place they are in right now; then take the positive qualities of the pretend place and bring them back to the present

Word Smart Students Can:

* read a book or write in a diary

Number Smart Students Can:

* make a chart of the good and bad things that are happening, and think about how the bad things could be changed into plusses

Nature Smart Students Can:

* pretend to be in the woods, waiting quietly for a deer to come; become aware of the physical changes that could be elicited inside while they wait, then bring the same sensations to the present setting

People Smart Students Can:

* think about writing a letter to a friend or pen pal about what they are learning and how well it's been accomplished; how much can they share with a friend about what is being learned or being done right now?

* concentrate on learning what they can to share more with others, then write a letter to get a friend's advice about how to not be bored

The Learning Process

Teachers and parents can only do so much in making learning happen. They can determine what should be learned, and try to support the learning through structure and reinforcement. Ultimately, however, the responsibility for learning must be the student's. This section is devoted to strategies and associations that learners can develop and implement independently, once they understand how they can make learning happen for themselves.

Getting Ready for Homework

What will help students most when they get ready to do their homework? Where should they do it? What should they have around them?

Music Smart Students Can:

* have the kind of music or sounds in the background that promotes concentration for them

Picture Smart Students Can:

* have pictures or charts around that would help provide mental stimulation

Body Smart Students Can:

* have all the physical supplies needed within arm's reach

Self Smart Students Can:

* arrange study space so that it feels comfortable

Word Smart Students Can:

* make a list of the things that need to be done, then post the list with written comments on each item when completed ("nice job," "well done," etc.)

Number Smart Students Can:

* figure out how much time each thing will take, and plan time for breaks; then set goals for the homework session and apportion a reward for each completed task

Nature Smart Students Can:

* look over the study space, and include things that create a sense of ease; be sure the lighting is appropriate for the task

People Smart Students Can:

* think about how much help is wanted or needed, then ask who can be solicited for help, if it is needed

Making Memory Mindful

Sometimes students need to be mindful in order to remember things. This means carefully thinking about which Smart Part they are going to use in order to store this information. Here are different ways to make memories work better.

Music Smart Students Can:

* use music or rhythm to help remember something
* think of examples of things learned using music
* create a rap or a beat using the information that needs to be remembered

Picture Smart Students Can:

* ask, "What is the 'big picture'?"
* use a mental camera to take a picture and remember it for future review

Body Smart Students Can:

* recall, "What personal hands-on experiences have I had that I can connect to this?"
* ask, "How can I connect this to something similar from the world of games or sports?"

Self Smart Students Can:

* ask, "Why am I learning this? How could it be helpful to me?"
* think, "How can I connect it to something that I already know?"

Word Smart Students Can:

* list vocabulary or synonyms that relate to the information to be remembered
* ask, "How can I *paraphrase* and summarize?"

Number Smart Students Can:

* ask, "What are the key questions and topics in this field? Which are more important? What is the essential information?"
* reflect, "How can I better organize this information?"

Nature Smart Students Can:

* ask, "What is something I know about nature that I can connect to this?"

People Smart Students Can:

* predict, "What is the author likely to say next?"
* ask, "How could I retell this to younger children so that they would remember it?"

Trying to Remember Anything

What was it that the students were supposed to remember to do after school today? What did they need to bring home? They often need to remember things but don't have a piece of paper handy to write them down. Here are some strategies they can try, using all of their Smart Parts.

Music Smart Students Can:

* use music or rhythm as a memory aid; think of examples of things learned using music
* create a rap or a beat using the information to be remembered

Picture Smart Students Can:

* create a graphic organizer that has all the elements of what is to be remembered
* visualize what is to be remembered, then put it into a mental movie or a mental picture

Body Smart Students Can:

* review the material while exercising
* build something out of LEGOs or pipe cleaners that represents what is to be remembered
* put the information on a piece of paper, then cut it up and rebuild it

Self Smart Students Can:

* think about the feelings inspired regarding what they are trying to remember; ask, "How can I make it relevant to my goals, ambitions, or priorities?" and then connect it to an emotion or a personal thought

Word Smart Students Can:

* create a first-letter mnemonic or an anagram with the information
* write a "story" embedding the information (e.g., *Tooth and Nail* approach, using SAT words, etc.) in the plot

Number Smart Students Can:

* analyze what needs to be remembered, isolating what they know from what they don't know
* categorize the information into groups, then chunk things into smaller parts

Nature Smart Students Can:

* use the natural environment to help remember information, relating subject matter to knowledge of plants or animals
* create an analogy from the natural world

People Smart Students Can:

* think about familiar people or characters whom they've met in reading
* connect the information being remembered to people; group and/or sort by types of people who might use this information in the work world
* think about how the information could be taught to someone of a different culture

Organizing a Desk

Clean up your desk! Clean your room! Adults always want children to keep things orderly. They want students to organize; they want things to look neat. Here are some ideas that students can use to keep their desks organized.

Music Smart Students Can:

* think of the desk as sheet music: the books are the lyrics, the pencils are the music, and the paper is the music's notation. Each subject in school is a measure, and the student's personal items (toys, calendar, etc.) represent the theme. Make sure all the parts blend but are still separate, like a favorite piece of music

Picture Smart Students Can:

* take a photograph of their desk or book bag when it is in perfect condition, with everything in its place; post the photograph where it can be seen every day, and make sure the desk or book bag matches the picture

Body Smart Students Can:

* use small boxes, bins, individual folders, or small mesh bags for each type of item; when everything is put in its place, they have an ideal arrangement—nothing will fall or be out of place
* practice building an organized space by taking it apart and then rebuilding it to achieve recognition of where everything belongs without having to think about it

Self Smart Students Can:

* prioritize things in the desk according to preference and complexity of arrangement; organize the desk items from most favorite to least favorite, then draw a

smiley face to post on the most favorite side and a sad
face to post on the least favorite side

Word Smart Students Can:

* label materials to be organized and then label the parts
  of the desk accordingly; match the items to the labels
  whenever returning things to their correct spot
* write a personal note and put it someplace where it
  will be retrieved
* write sticky notes to remind themselves where the
  unusual things have been deposited

Number Smart Students Can:

* make a numbered list of things that need organization, then number the same parts on the desk; put the
  things in order according to the list
* create a rating sheet to grade daily how organized the
  desk is

Nature Smart Students Can:

* think of a favorite animal and ask, "How does that
  animal become organized? How does it store things?
  Where does it find the things it needs?"

People Smart Students Can:

* think of an acquaintance who is very organized,
  then interview that person about planning where to
  put things; identify how you can be like that person;
  finally, ask that person to watch as you sort things and
  organize them, giving hints on how to do it better

Remembering Chores

What is the best way to remember chores? After students have tried these methods a few times, they might find that they can remember to do them on their own.

Music Smart Students Can:

   * set an alarm with an agreeable, identifiable ring
   * have someone call on a cell phone that plays a specific ringtone as a reminder

Picture Smart Students Can:

   * take a photograph of themselves doing chores, then mount the photo somewhere it will be seen often, such as under a clock or on the refrigerator. Then, when viewed, it will draw attention to whether the chores have been done today

Body Smart Students Can:

   * think of a movement they do all the time (like twirling their hair or tapping their foot). Link that movement in their mind to the chores, so every time they do the movement they think about the chores and whether they are done

Self Smart Students Can:

   * ask, "What reasons do I have to do my chores? How will I feel when they are done? What will I feel like if I don't do them?"

Word Smart Students Can:

   * write a reminder note and post it in a convenient spot

Number Smart Students Can:

* list the pros and cons of doing the chores, then ask, "What are the consequences of each?"

* reflect, "How can I be more efficient?"

Nature Smart Students Can:

* theorize, "How can my pet help me do the chores, or remind me to do them?"

People Smart Students Can:

* do chores with a friend

* have a friend call as a reminder

* think of ways to spend more time with friends, as long as the chores are finished first

Word Problems

Here are several suggestions to figure out how to solve word problems, when words alone don't work.

Music Smart Students Can:

* listen to the words and wonder, "Which ones should be read loudest, softest, in the highest pitch?"

* pick an instrument to represent the "math" words, and whenever they hear or see a "math" word in the story, play that instrument in their head

Picture Smart Students Can:

* draw the story, or make it into a storyboard to see the sequence of events; if the story is an addition or multiplication story, the storyboard frames could get bigger, and if it is a subtraction or division problem, the frames could get smaller

Body Smart Students Can:

* convert the story into movements to be acted out or pantomimed

* "build" the story with pipe cleaners, LEGOs, or attribute blocks

Self Smart Students Can:

* reflect, "What would this problem feel like to me? Can I place myself in the problem? If I was one of the 'items' mentioned in the problem, would I be getting bigger or smaller?"

* rewrite the problem, making it more relevant to personal experience

Word Smart Students Can:

* think of other words that could be used to rewrite the story problem; add some descriptors that would make the story come alive

* ask, "What other vocabulary could I use that would help this story make sense?"

Number Smart Students Can:

* convert the story into numbers, then come up with a formula for solving the problem

* ask, "What other problem is this like?"

Nature Smart Students Can:

* convert the word problem into a story about a favorite animal

* categorize it: "Is it like something else I have already done or seen?"

People Smart Students Can:

   * ask, "Who would need to know about this kind of thinking?"
   * theorize: "How would a scientist approach this problem?"
   * teach someone else in class how to solve the problem

Learning Vocabulary

The following prompts will help students to make associations that will help them remember key vocabulary words.

Music Smart Students Can:

   * ask, "What music or sound pattern comes to mind?"
   * ask, "What lyrics or song titles remind me of this?"
   * identify a type of music that mentally connects to the word

Picture Smart Students Can:

   * associate the word with a color or shape
   * create a mental picture of the word

Body Smart Students Can:

   * associate the word with a physical movement
   * ask, "What action reminds me of this concept?"
   * think of an analogy from the world of sports

Self Smart Students Can:

   * relate the word to a feeling
   * ask, "What reflective process would I connect to this?"
   * connect the word to a personal value

Word Smart Students Can:

* relate the word to a story or a poem
* think of five descriptors for the word
* ask, "What print materials would I want to use with this?"

Number Smart Students Can:

* wonder, "What number or quantity comes to mind when I hear this word?"
* ask, "How can I measure this?"
* create a formula that expresses the vocabulary term

Nature Smart Students Can:

* relate the word to a plant or animal
* make an analogy between the word and a concept in the natural world
* ask, "What scientific principle do I think of when I think of this word or concept?"

People Smart Students Can:

* think, "What famous person do I associate with this word?"
* ask, "What movie or book character comes to mind?"
* relate this to any group of people or a culture

Decoding Words

Here are a few supplemental activities that students could consider when differentiating reading instruction at the elementary level.

Music Smart Students Can:

* think, "What does this word sound like?"
* ask, "Can I think of a song that uses this word?"
* create a jingle or rap for this word
* sing the letters in order

Picture Smart Students Can:

* imagine creating a huge neon sign or billboard for this word; what would they want it to look like?
* move the shapes around using plastic letters, and build something memorable; what does it look like?
* take the parts of the word that are difficult and underline them in a bright color, or highlight the difficult part to see it more easily in the mind's eye

Body Smart Students Can:

* ask, "What physical movement do I associate with this word?"
* build the word out of Scrabble tiles
* use their fingers or hands to form the letters
* write the word on the white board in big letters, then in small letters
* build the word out of pipe cleaners

Self Smart Students Can:

* ask, "What feeling do I associate with this word?"
* make the word funny, silly, or unique, taking time to make a personal connection to the word
* wonder, "How can I be truly mindful about this word?"

Word Smart Students Can:

* find the root word, or the small word inside the big word
* ask, "What is this word in another language?"
* look for a word that means the same thing, even though it may look different

Number Smart Students Can:

* count how many letters are in the word
* identify the most difficult letter sequence in this word, and come up with a strategy to remember this order
* reflect upon whether there exist other word families that exhibit an identical letter combination; what is the pattern?

Nature Smart Students Can:

* think of something in nature that can be related to this word
* connect the word to a plant or animal, or something in the natural environment
* make the word out of leaves, grass, or flower petals

People Smart Students Can:

* think of a movie character who might use the word

* ask, "Why does the author use this word instead of a different word?"

* think about how they might teach this word to someone else; how would this technique be employed?

Reading Comprehension

Students understand a story better when they use their Smart Parts.

Music Smart Students Can:

* listen to the sounds of the voices in the story

* if listening to someone else reading the story aloud, ask themselves, "By really listening to the characters, am I better able to understand the story?"

Picture Smart Students Can:

* let the words help draw a mental picture. How does the character look? What about the background? What colors do they see? What shapes? What words did the author use that made the picture strong? If they change the words into a mental picture, is it easier to understand what is read?

Body Smart Students Can:

* act out what is happening, using their bodies to convert words into movements or actions

Self Smart Students Can:

   * think about how the story makes them feel; does it make them happy, sad, excited, angry, or interested?

Word Smart Students Can:

   * rewrite the story using their own words
   * take one sentence and change each word without entirely changing the meaning
   * make the story stronger or sillier (in order to do this, they have to understand it)

Number Smart Students Can:

   * make a list of the things that happen in the story, then number them in sequence

Nature Smart Students Can:

   * imagine that the location of the story is now in a jungle, then ask, "How would this change the story?"

People Smart Students Can:

   * think of a peer who is reminiscent of one of the characters in the story; how are the two alike and how are they different?

Visualization Skills

When students read to themselves, they need to be able to connect to the story in order to understand it. Many people turn what they read into a picture in their heads, which they can see as if they were watching a movie. Not everyone is good at visualizing without assistance. However, children can learn to visualize by tapping their Smart Parts.

Music Smart Students Can:

* listen to different music and visualize a character or an action that the music triggers, then draw squiggly lines while listening to different kinds of music; compare the images that were created—did they change?

Picture Smart Students Can:

* listen to an action story with their eyes closed, then draw, paint, or photograph an image in their mind's eye

Body Smart Students Can:

* visualize a pleasant activity (e.g., swimming, fishing, skiing, playing football, walking in the woods)

Self Smart Students Can:

* think, "When I think of 'happy,' what color do I think of? What shape reminds me of being sad?"

Word Smart Students Can:

* imagine the cover of a favorite book, then read the words on it; then open to a page in the middle of the book and focus on a specific word; make the word bigger and read it

Number Smart Students Can:

* ask, "What is something I do that has an order or sequence?" Mentally review that sequence (e.g., baking cookies, brushing one's teeth, or playing a favorite video game) and imagine a clock in the background. What time does the student start? What time does the student finish? Focus on seeing the clock

Nature Smart Students Can:

* picture themselves in a favorite location outdoors, thinking about the plants, air, sky, and ground; how much detail can they add to the picture?

People Smart Students Can:

* visualize someone they have not seen in a long time; see the person's face, making it clear and up-close
* visualize a character from a story or book

Assessment

Assessments should be designed so that all students can demonstrate the knowledge and thinking skills targeted by the lesson or unit. In a differentiated classroom, students should be given choices about the type of assessment they would like to complete.

An Example

If you are doing a unit on urbanization with fourth graders, for example, you might have the following learning outcomes in mind:

- ✓ the growth of cities
- ✓ how industrialization led to urban growth
- ✓ how immigration has affected cities
- ✓ how transportation has changed cities
- ✓ how cities influence our economy
- ✓ how cities support us culturally (music, art, museums, literature, etc.)
- ✓ the positive effects of cities
- ✓ the negative effects of cities
- ✓ what big cities are like today

Here are a few sample projects that students could complete in order to demonstrate their understanding of the concept of urbanization. The teacher could assign these or give students their choice.

Music Smart Students Can:

* burn a CD that includes songs, parts of songs, or sound effects of the city; make sure that the choices show an understanding of urbanization, immigration, transportation, positive and negative effects of cities, and what is happening to cities today

Picture Smart Students Can:

* create a mural or a storyboard that shows understanding of the urbanization concepts described above

Body Smart Students Can:

* build a model that demonstrates urbanization concepts

Self Smart Students Can:

* describe how it would feel to be an immigrant coming to America in the mid-1800s; share their thoughts in the form of a personal journal, and make sure to include observations about urbanization

Word Smart Students Can:

* write a newspaper article about the growth of the city in which they live, and how it relates to the concepts of urbanization and immigration discussed in class, including how transportation has made a difference in the history of the city

Number Smart Students Can:

* create a time line of the important events/elements in the history of urbanization and include milestones of immigration and transportation, and the current era; chart population changes

Nature Smart Students Can:

* compare the natural environment before urbanization to the environment after, including information about local plants and animals, and how they have been affected, both positively and negatively

People Smart Students Can:

* interview several senior citizens (perhaps using an interview form) about their own experiences related to urbanization, immigration, and the growth of transportation; ask them about the positive and negative effects of cities in their lives, and what they think about cities today; then write or tape-record their answers

Rubric

In order to use these MI alternatives successfully, the teacher must provide students with a rubric that clearly spells out the learning outcomes required.

Create the following rubric so that you and the students (and their parents) know what you want communicated, regardless of which of the assessment alternatives they choose. Give students a time frame for completion of the project, and tell them how much time they will be given to share their project with the class.

RUBRIC ON URBANIZATION PROJECT

Learning outcomes being measured	Included accurately, shows depth of understanding and creative interpretation 3	Included and shows some understanding of the information 2	Is mentioned but shows little understanding of the material 1	Not included 0
The relationship between the growth of factories and the growth of cities				
The relationship between immigration and the growth of cities				
How changes in transportation led to changes in cities				
Positive and negative effects of large cities				
What is happening today in our cities				

Tic-Tac-Do

Some teachers use a Tic-Tac-Toe board to present assessment alternatives to students, called a *Tic-Tac-Do.*

For this assignment, the student must pick three items from the Tic-Tac-Do board below. The student may do them in any order, and may work across, down, or diagonally. A student who uses the Wild Card must substitute another activity that meets the criterion of demonstrating knowledge about the topic the class has been studying. It is *not* a "free" space.

TIC-TAC-DO TEMPLATE

Make up an anagram for _____.	Write a song with lyrics to _____.	Interview a person who _____.
Develop a time line for _____.	**WILD CARD**	Connect _____ to a plant or animal.
Create a picture summarizing _____.	Think of a time when _____ was important to you.	What physical activity do you associate with _____?

Evaluation Grid

Most school districts provide structured approaches to support teachers in how a curriculum is taught at each grade level. Often, teachers become so focused on the content of what they are teaching that they lose sight of the strategies they are trying to reinforce in students for them to become independent learners.

A learning strategy

a)   includes a general approach to solving a set of problems;

b)   promotes goal-directed behavior;

c)   teaches a selection of appropriate procedures;

d)   guides implementation of a procedure;

e)   shows how to monitor progress;

f)   can be controlled;

g)   provides and focuses on cues to take action (Institute for Research in Learning Disabilities, 1990a, pp. 15, 21)

Most teachers already incorporate a variety of intelligences into their lessons. One way to become more aware of the strategies you are currently using, and the intelligences you are incorporating, is to use an MI Strategies Grid. To use it, read the professional literature on a specific approach or strategy, and determine which intelligences are being highlighted. This will give you a clearer insight into matching specific strategies to specific students.

A sample grid is shown here, exploring a variety of reading strategies.

MI STRATEGY GRID

STRATEGIES	(wave icon)	(triangle/A icon)	(hands icon)	(bird/music icon)	(ABC block icon)	(3-2=xy icon)	(lotus icon)	(running people icon)
Reading: Word Identification								
Picture clues		x						
Semantic clues				x	x			
Structural analysis					x	x		
Phonic analysis	x				x			
Orton-Gillingham		x	x		x	x		
DISSECT						x	x	
Word wall		x	x		x			
Sight word bingo		x	x		x			x
Silly stories				x	x			x
Visual configuration		x			x			
Wilson	x	x	x	x	x	x		

MI STRATEGY GRID (CONTINUED)

STRATEGIES	(music)	(triangle)	(hands)	(nature)	(ABC)	(3-2-1 xy)	(leaf)	(people)
Reading: Word Comprehension								
Brainstorming								x
K-W-L				x		x		
PreQuest				x		x		
Story mapping		x						
Repeated reading	x				x			x
Choral rehearsal	x		x					x
Paraphrasing					x			
PreP						x		
QAR						x		
RAP strategy	x				x			

4

HIGHER-LEVEL
THINKING SKILLS

In today's standards-based environment, teachers are looking for ways to help children to transfer information and skills so that they can problem-solve in a variety of contexts and situations. Some people have difficulty understanding how MI could be useful in this process. This brief chapter relates a variety of higher-level thinking prompts to MI, and gives specific ways that children can learn to do this on their own.

Hutch was a third-grade student who always focused on the facts and the details. When she had new vocabulary words to learn, she would memorize the definitions word for word right off the page. She did well on tests where the wording on the test was the same as the wording on the worksheet, but when she got to end-of-year or state assessments, she scored much lower than she did on weekly classroom tests. The wording was different, and she did not realize what was being asked. When we did reading comprehension activities, she could not seem to identify the main idea, especially if it was not explicitly stated in the text. She would repeat the details, but could not understand how to progress to more abstract thinking.

Hutch was a visual/spatial learner. She remembered details because she could "see" the details in her head. She would look at the words and convert them into snapshots of the setting or clear images of the characters. When she recalled the information, she would relook at the pictures in her head and that would bring back the information. She was memorizing without really learning.

To help Hutch understand the difference between the detail and the main idea, we had her focus on the gestalt, the outside shape of the picture in her head, and not the detail. She learned to "look through a telescope rather than a microscope," so that she could imagine seeing things from a distance. After just a few examples like this, she was able to understand how to transition things from concrete to abstract. Telling her how to do this in words or in steps made no sense to her. However, when she was able to do it through her strengths—visually—the concept made perfect sense to her.

———

To develop higher-order thinking skills, read and reflect on the following strategies for asking questions of students with strengths in differing Smart Parts.

Music Smart thinkers find it easy to answer questions when the words below are embedded in the questions. These words trigger connections to patterns of sound, songs, rhythms, tempo, or auditory tone changes.

* Sounds like . . .
* Listen . . .
* Do you hear . . . ?
* Reverberate
* Resonance
* Noise or sound level

Picture Smart thinkers find it easy to answer questions when the words below are embedded in the questions. These words trigger the creation of visual images or spatial relationships.

* Imagine . . .
* Visualize . . .
* Show . . .
* Reverse . . .
* A different perspective . . .
* Your point of view . . .

Body Smart thinkers find it easy to answer questions when the words below are embedded in the questions. These words and other active verbs trigger connections to physical actions, movements, or activities.

* Backtracking for a minute . . .
* A connecting idea is . . .
* Take action to . . .

Self Smart thinkers find it easy to answer questions when the words below are embedded in the questions. These words trigger personal feelings, values, and opinions.

* The best part . . .
* On the positive side . . .
* An interesting part is . . .
* The best part is . . .
* I really liked . . .
* What if . . . ?
* I predict . . .
* I wonder . . .

* It is important that . . .
* The worst . . .
* Why . . .

Word Smart thinkers find it easy to answer questions when the words below are embedded in the questions. These words trigger connections to words, whether written or oral.

* How would you say . . . ?
* In other words, . . .
* A title . . .
* Rephrase . . .
* The language . . .

Number Smart thinkers find it easy to answer questions when the words below are embedded in the questions. These words trigger measuring, comparing, figuring, or cause-and-effect.

* Compare . . .
* Categorize . . .
* Determining the positives and negatives . . .
* Combine . . .
* Suppose . . .
* If _____ , then . . .
* The results of . . .
* In contrast, . . .
* Take a small part like . . .
* Similarly, . . .
* By contrast, . . .
* How about . . .

Nature Smart thinkers find it easy to answer questions when the words below are embedded in the questions. These words trigger connections to the worlds of plants, of animals, or of the natural environment.

* Naturally . . .
* Outdoors . . .
* Any phrase referring to a plant or animal or using metaphors or similes from nature: "That is in the ozone!" "Out of this world!" "This is like a hen house." "He is denser than fog." "The cat is out of the bag."

People Smart thinkers find it easy to answer the following types of questions or respond to these words that are embedded in the questions. These words trigger connections to others.

* Other perspectives . . .
* We can . . .
* A group . . .
* The culture . . .
* Members . . .
* Several people . . .

GLOSSARY

Arrays: Items grouped by categories.

Assistive technology: Any tool, usually electronic, that allows the learner to accomplish a task that may be otherwise problematic, like a spell checker, grammar checker, voice-activated software, or tape recorder.

Automaticity: Learning something so that you can retrieve it quickly and use it at the automatic level, without much thought (e.g., knowing that $3 \times 3 = 9$).

Bibliotherapy: Using books with strong social or psychological themes as safe avenues for children to deal with difficult feelings or issues in their lives.

Brainstorming: A process of activating prior knowledge. It can be recorded in a list, a graphic organizer, or done verbally.

Bubble maps: Graphic organizers using circles for key words. Size and color of circles may designate level or hierarchy of the words.

Choral reading: Reading aloud in unison with others.

Chunking: A process of grouping things together in order to compress them so that they are easier to remember.

Circle of friends: A meeting whose purpose is for all members to offer support to one member who is having difficulty. Members brainstorm ideas or make commitments to help.

Class meeting: A structured gathering of the entire class to discuss an issue or problem, formalized by William Glasser.

Cloze passage: Writing a paragraph or short article with specific words left blank, so that the reader has to fill in the blanks. This is often used as an assessment for comprehension.

Concept map: A graphic organizer that relates to a specific concept, often used as a brainstorming technique.

Connections chart: A T-chart graphically depicting the learner's past experiences related to the topic, compared to concrete knowledge gleaned from outside personal experience.

Compacting: A process where a unit can be compressed so a student with strong background knowledge can "test out" of the daily assignments or homework, instead working on an independent project for depth of knowledge.

Contract for learning: A written, formal agreement for improving student learning or behavior. The student is an equal partner in the development of the contract.

Cornell note-taking method: An approach through which students take and analyze notes for greater understanding. It was developed by Walter Paulk at Cornell University. Students draw a vertical line 2 ½ inches from the left-hand margin, and another horizontally, 2 inches from the bottom. To the right of the vertical line, students take notes in whatever form suits them. Immediately after the note-taking session, they write questions in the left column; the material in the right column is the correct answer. The questions can be at any level in Bloom's taxonomy. The line at the bottom designates space to be used to write a summary sentence that includes key words from the questions above.

Developmental sequence: The order in which most children naturally learn various skills or patterns.

Diary: A record of personal thoughts, feelings, or events.

Differentiated instruction: A process through which different students are honored for their different ways of learning. Classrooms can be differentiated in many ways, including by readiness (different books for students at different levels), by interest (pick a topic that appeals to you), or by product (varying projects that provide opportunities to share what is learned), and by learning style or multiple intelligence. In the twenty-first century, this approach is becoming very popular in the United States.

Discovery method: A way of teaching concepts through which the teacher provides information and ample experiences for students to discover a pattern or concept. This is most often seen in math or science classes.

Elaboration: A process whereby students expand on their ideas by adding more description.

Fernald approach: A specific structured way to learn words using a combination of student interest, tracing while saying the word, remembering the word, and keeping it in an organized filing system to be used later. It uses VAKT (Visual, Auditory, Kinesthetic, and Tactile) modalities.

5 W's and H: A structured approach to writing that asks students to respond to the cues who, what, where, when, why, and how.

Focused free write: Giving a prompt after which students are to write continuously about the prompt for a stated amount of time. This is stream of consciousness writing, so spelling and grammar do not count.

Freewriting: Automatic writing usually done as an exercise.

Generalization: Taking facts or details and categorizing, abstracting, or inferring from the details.

Glass analysis: A method of teaching reading in which a variety of first consonants are added to a set ending (such as, _and: sand, land, stand).

Graphic organizer: A visual map or structure used to organize information to make it easier to understand and to show how various layers are connected.

Group write: A method of composing a written work where several students brainstorm ways in which to write it; the finished product contains words and ideas from all participants.

Guided reading: Reading with the help of guided questions, either written or oral, that help the reader target what is important.

Impress reading: Repeating exactly what someone else reads while looking at the written word.

Inquiry: A method of teaching in which the teacher poses a solution and students figure out the topic or concept by asking questions or doing research.

I Spy: A game whereby one person gives clues that can be seen in the environment while others try to guess the object being described.

Journaling: Writing on a topic the teacher determines.

K-W-L: A three-column chart used to organize prior knowledge (K), what you want to learn (W), and what you have learned (L). It is often used to get students to tap into their prior knowledge about something that they are going to learn.

Life space interview: A technique of interviewing students to help them analyze a behavioral incident immediately after it happens to generate options and solutions; developed by David Wineman and William Morris and refined by Nicholas Long and Mary Wood.

Lindamood: Commercially available phonemic analysis materials.

Literature circle: Structured discussions about a book or story. Writing is tied to the literature that is read.

Matrix: A way of analyzing a product by attaching levels to standards of achievement.

Meditation: A technique used to relax and become self-aware that includes controlled breathing and conscious focusing.

Metacognition: A learner's awareness of his or her own thinking.

Mind Mapping: A graphic organizer that integrates words and pictures, developed by Tony Buzan.

Mnemonic: A strategy that aids memory. It can be a connection through any intelligence.

Networking: A graphic organizer that teaches students the relationship between various words; developed by Gary Long and others at the National Technical Institute for the Deaf.

Neuro-linguistic programming: An intervention technique that helps people reframe experiences to perceive them in a more positive way and give individuals a greater sense of control over memories and negative emotions; developed by Richard Bandler and others.

Orton-Gillingham: A multisensory approach to teaching reading and spelling developed for students with learning disabilities.

Paraphrasing: Restating an idea in your own words.

Peer mediation: A process of involving students in listening to peer conflicts and helping to solve them.

Phonemic analysis: A highly structured approach to understanding relationships between sounds and symbols.

Phonological awareness: Understanding and using sounds and sound patterns to build words and language.

Picture association technique: Using a key picture to help the student identify a word.

Prereading: Specific ways to prepare for increasing understanding of a passage or a book by triggering knowledge before the reading begins. This may consist of previewing vocabulary, using bold print or pictures, or skimming questions at the end.

Prewriting: The thinking process required to organize thoughts prior to doing a writing assignment.

QAR: Question–answer relationship. A strategy that allows students to identify where answers are located (in the book, in your head, requiring inferences, etc.).

Reciprocal teaching: A method to teach reading comprehension in which students pair up, one reads while the other listens and generates questions, then they discuss and switch roles.

Repeated reading: Repeating the same passage or phrase or page until the student has reached fluency, with no pauses or miscues.

Round-robin stories: Each person adds a sentence or a word to language started by someone else, until everyone has had a chance to add to it.

Scaffolding: A process of teaching skills in incremental steps with enough support that the student is always successful; requires a high degree of task analysis by the teacher.

Scared straight: A model of preventing misbehavior in which convicted felons and drug abusers tell personal stories to young children to scare them away from crime and drug abuse.

Self-advocacy: Communication from the learner sharing strategies or teaching approaches that would aid in the learning.

Semantic map: A graphic organizer of language. There are many different types, depending on the way the information needs to be organized.

Sequence cards: Using pictures or phrases or sentences to show the difference between past, present, and future, or to demonstrate the sequence of events.

Shadowing: A method of teaching in which students spend time with another person at a place of employment to see whether they would like it as a potential job or career.

Slotting: A method of writing in which the writer substitutes a variety of words in place of the original, and then decides which one to use in the finished product.

Storyboard: A visual organizer often used to organize thoughts for a video or movie.

Story map: A structured graphic organizer with two columns, one for cause and the other for effect. The teacher tiers the activity by filling in as much as is needed in order for the student to be successful. With successive use, the teacher would leave more blanks for the student to fill in.

Strategy: A systematic approach to mastering a skill or content. A strategy can be applied to more than one piece of information.

Think-Pair-Share: A specific structure used to get more students involved in reflection on what was just presented. Two students are matched up as partners, and periodically, through the lesson, the teacher asks them to think about what was just said, pair up with their partner, and share what they think it means.

Tic-Tac-Do: An activity choice sheet allowing for differentiation of assignments students can do to demonstrate skill or knowledge of a topic.

Tiering: Taking the same task or information and amending it by readiness level so that a variety of students can be successful.

Venn diagram: A visual organizer used for comparisons and contrasts.

Whole Language: An approach to teaching reading and writing based on a whole-to-part structure, focusing more on meaning than mechanics.

Wilson program: A highly structured multisensory reading program that incorporates tapping, phonemic awareness, counting syllables, mouth movements necessary for sounds, and symbols for blending sounds into words.

BIBLIOGRAPHY

Armstrong, Thomas. *Multiple Intelligences in the Classroom*, 2d ed. Alexandria, VA: Association for Supervision and Curriculum, 2000.

———. *The Multiple Intelligences of Reading and Writing: Making the Words Come Alive*. Alexandria, VA: Association for Supervision and Curriculum, 2003.

Arnold, Ellen. *Brilliant Brain Becomes Brainy!* Rochester, NY: Arncraft, 1997.

———. *MI Strategies for Kids: Teachers Manual*. Chicago: Zephyr Press, 2000. Set Includes: *Brilliant Brain Banishes Boredom, Brilliant Brain Battles Bad Guys, Brilliant Brain Selects Spelling Strategies, Magnificent Mind Listens Mindfully, Magnificent Mind Magnifies Meaning When Reading,* and *Magnificent Mind Masters Multiplication*.

———. *Master Mountain Snow Sports*. Rochester, NY: Arncraft, 2005.

Bos, Candace, and Sharon Vaughn. *Strategies for Teaching Students with Learning and Behavior Problems*, 6th ed. Boston: Allyn & Bacon, 2006.

Bruce, Barbara. *7 Ways of Teaching the Bible to Children*. Nashville, TN: Abingdon Press, 1996.

———. *Mental Aerobics: 75 Ways to Keep Your Brain Fit*. Nashville, TN: Abingdon Press, 2004.

Campbell, Don. *The Mozart Effect: Tapping the Power of Music to Heal the Body, Strengthen the Mind, and Unlock the Creative Spirit*. New York: Avon, 1997.

Gardner, Howard. *Creating Minds: An Anatomy of Creativity Seen Through the Lives of Freud, Einstein, Picasso, Stravinsky, Eliot, Graham, and Gandhi.* New York: Basic Books, 1993.

———. *Intelligence Reframed: Multiple Intelligences for the 21st Century.* New York: Basic Books, 1999.

———. *The Disciplined Mind: What All Students Should Understand.* New York: Simon & Schuster, 1999.

Gerber, Paul, and Henry Reiff. *Speaking for Themselves: Ethnographic Interviews with Adults with Learning Disabilities.* Ann Arbor, MI: University of Michigan Press, 1991.

Goleman, Daniel. *Emotional Intelligence: 10th Anniversary Edition; Why It Can Matter More Than IQ.* New York: Bantam, 2006.

Healy, Jane. *Endangered Minds: Why Children Don't Think—and What We Can Do About It.* New York: Simon & Schuster, 1999.

Langer, Ellen. *Mindfulness.* Reading, MA: Addison-Wesley, 1989.

Levine, Mel. *Educational Care: A System for Understanding and Helping Children with Learning Differences at Home and in School,* 2nd ed. Cambridge, MA: Educators Publishing Service, 2002.